Essential Enrichment

Charlotte Garner

Copyright

Disclaimer

The content included within this book is for informational purposes only, and it should not be used to substitute advice from qualified veterinary professionals with regard to potential illnesses or diseases. Any specific situation that may arise with your own dog should be considered on an individual basis under the advice of a relevantly qualified practitioner. The use of this book implies your acceptance of this disclaimer.

Table of Contents

Introduction

Lots of dogs show undesirable behaviours. Barking, digging, chewing, howling, endless sniffing, destroying your possessions or furniture, separation anxiety, and hyperactivity to name but a few. However, it's important that we understand that there is always a reason behind these behaviours. Your dog does not behave this way intentionally, out of naughtiness, or simply to annoy you!

Many owners feel frustrated when their dog is constantly digging up the garden and sending their flowers flying yet again. As soon as they have planted new plants, their dog comes along and rips them out. Wasting their hard-earned money and time in the process and leaving them with another mess to clean up.

Or when owners come home to discover their sofa has been chewed up again, or there are more teeth marks on their dining table. They are left with trying to repair or replace their furniture once more, only adding to their frustration and expense.

Some owners are exhausted trying to manage their dog's energy levels and tire them out. They are walking further and playing for longer, yet still their dog seems wired and hyperactive. The owners can't understand what they are doing wrong, they are worn out while their dog seems to have more energy than ever!

I have been in all of these scenarios with my own dogs and can fully understand the stress it can bring to your life and the damage it can do to the relationship you share with your dog in the process. I felt out of control, frustrated, and powerless over my dog's behaviour because I didn't know how to help them.

This all changed when I found out the benefits of enrichment. Suddenly, it was like a weight had been lifted from my shoulders. I learned what my dog's needs truly were and how I could help to fulfil them. Their problem behaviours became a thing of the past because they now had an outlet for their natural desires.

The great news is, the information you will find in this book, will help you to reach this point too. The relationship you share with your dog will be improved, and their behaviour problems will become a distant memory. Enrichment was the missing link to my dog's happiness, and it is likely to be the same for your dog too.

In this book you will learn:

- How encouraging your dog's freedom of choice can help to increase their confidence
- What enrichment really is and how you can use it effectively to improve your dog's life
- How enrichment can benefit both your dog and yourself, and increase the bond you share with each other

- How enrichment can help to reduce your dog's problem behaviours
- What types of enrichment activity would be most enjoyable for your dog to take part in
- How to intertwine enrichment into your dog's daily life with ease, making it sustainable and providing long-lasting results
- Answers to some frequently asked questions and queries about enrichment
- Over 50+ fantastic enrichment activities for you to try with your own dog

So, if a relaxed, contented, canine companion sounds like just what you need, let's get started!

The Freedom Of Choice

Although this book is centred around enrichment, I feel this chapter deserves to be the first thing you read. Here we will look at the importance of allowing and encouraging your dog to have the freedom of choice. This is known more formally as giving them 'agency,' and refers to encouraging your dog to have control over their actions and the resulting effects these actions have on their environment. Although this may sound a little complicated, hopefully I can explain it in a way that you can fully understand and appreciate.

What Is Agency?

In the canine world, we define agency as giving your dog the opportunity to control their actions and, in turn, the consequences of them. Our dogs are micro-managed and controlled by humans in almost every aspect of their lives. They have very few opportunities to do things that they want to do because their lives are often taken over by doing things that suit their human's needs. We control their diet, their exercise, the amount of attention they receive, their social interactions, their health care, and the situations they are put in, along with every other part of their life as a whole. A classic example is when you see a dog being dragged away from an interesting smell. When you consider the sheer importance of sniffing and scent to our dogs, it's a certainty that given the choice, they would want to take a good sniff of this exciting smell. Yet, all too often, their owner's hurry them along and physically pull them away and stop them interacting with their environment in the process. This is a real-life example of humans removing the very little agency our dogs have over their lives, when instead, they should be actively encouraging it.

Why Is Agency Important?
Providing your dog with agency in their life helps to increase their confidence levels because they feel more in control of their environment and what is happening to them, and around them. It can also reduce their stress and anxiety levels because they have the freedom to remove themselves from a situation that worries them. Although our dogs are domesticated pets, it's not uncommon for them to find themselves in homes that are unsuitable for meeting their needs and keeping them happy. For example, a Border Collie from working bloodlines would unlikely choose to home themselves in a busy, noisy, family home. They may struggle with this hectic lifestyle, but they have no option but to do the best they can because they have no choice, or agency, over this decision.

So, increasing the amount of agency your dog has over their environment and life is an essential part of their happiness and well-being.

What Does Agency Have To Do With Enrichment?
Enrichment is one of the ways that we can provide our dogs with more agency in their lives. Offering activities that your dog can choose to participate in,

instead of things they are forced to do, increases their agency over these scenarios. Enrichment encourages humans to consider things from their dog's perspective so you can better meet their needs and desires, and provide an outlet for their natural behaviours. In turn, enrichment increases the amount of agency your dog has over their life which is an excellent, ethical thing to do. The two notions go hand in hand; enrichment activities help to increase your dog's level of agency and increased agency encourages further participation in enrichment activities and so on!

How Do I Give My Dog More Agency?
Now you hopefully understand what agency is and how important it is to your dog's well-being, it's time to look at some suggestions about how you increase the amount of agency your dog has. But first, it's important to understand that *agency depends on having at least 2 positive outcomes for your dog to choose from*. For example, let's say you offer your dog a plain, dried, biscuit treat. Your dog has two choices, eat the treat that is pretty boring to them, or have no treat at all. This is not giving them agency, or the freedom to choose, because one of these options results in an undesirable outcome (I.e. not having a treat). Instead, offer your dog that same biscuit in one hand, and a delicious, natural treat that they love in the other hand. Chances are they will pick the tastier treat, and this is an example of your dog having agency over their own choices. So, a realistic explanation of agency is this:

- Choosing between 2 bad things is NOT agency.
- Choosing between 1 bad thing and 1 good thing is NOT agency.
- Choosing between 2 good things IS agency.
- Choosing between 1 good thing and 1 great thing IS agency.

Giving your dog agency can be as simple or as complex as you make it. And it will look different for individual dogs too. For example, some dogs may prioritise having agency over the choice of toy they play with more than having agency over the route they take on walks. This is very much personal to each different dog, so try and actively look at the areas of their life that your dog likes to have choice over, and encourage it. This is another piece of the enrichment puzzle, because having this information can help you to tailor your dog's enrichment activities to better suit their own needs.

Some simple ideas to increase your dog's ability to choose could be:

- **Resting Places** - A choice of different comfortable resting places for them use, in different rooms of the house. This way your dog doesn't have to pick between being uncomfortable, yet close to you, (I.e. lying on the cold kitchen floor while you are cooking dinner) or comfortable and far away from you. (In their comfy bed in a different room of the house when they really would want to be near to you)

- **Toys** - Providing your dog with different toys to choose from. Their preference may differ depending on their mood so it's a great idea to have a different variety of toys for them to pick. Find two similar toys that you know your dog loves and let them decide which one they want to play with. Try to play with the toys in different ways too and take note which games your dog enjoys the most. Some dogs may prefer chase games, catching games, or seeking games for example. We will explore these options later on in the book.
- **Treats** – Giving your dog new, novel, interesting treats to try is a great way to give them agency. Food platters which we will mention later on, are ideal for this! Offer your dog multiple treats which they love and let them choose which snack they fancy in this moment.
- **Sniffing** – As we mentioned at the start of this chapter, letting your dog choose where to sniff is one of THE best things you can do to improve their level of choice and their mental well-being. Take a look at Sniffaris later on the book for some inspiration. You can also increase your dog's agency by letting them choose the route they would like to explore on their walks.
- **Problem-Solving** – Basic problem-solving exercises like snuffle mats, lickmats, hiding treats/toys, and scatter feeding are all really easy ways to increase your dog's agency and their confidence in the process. We will look at these activities in more detail later in the book.

Agency can also help to improve some more complex issues, which we will look at next. Here's what I mean:

Reactivity – Many dogs are what is known as 'reactive' towards certain triggers which may include; other dogs, people, other animals, vehicles etc. This means they show an 'over-the-top' reaction when in the presence of these triggers, which can often lead to barking, lunging, and growling. Now, despite what some people think, reactive behaviours usually stem from your dog feeling fearful, and not because they are aggressive. For example, Delta (my youngest dog) is reactive towards other dogs that she doesn't know. There is a long and complex history resulting in her reactivity, but regardless of the reasonings behind it, she struggles to interact with unknown dogs appropriately. So, remembering that Delta is showing this behaviour (barking and lunging) because of anxiety and fear, I can give her some choices:

- *Undesirable option for her:* Forcing her to interact with the unknown dog.
- *Slightly more desirable option for her, but still not one she would actively choose:* Sit and watch the dog as they walk past.
- *Most desirable option for her:* To create distance between her and the dog until she reaches a point where she feels safe.

Now because I know and understand that Delta would want to create space between herself and the other dog if she had full freedom to choose in this scenario, this is the option we pick. She is not able to fully execute this on her own, because she would be on a lead in this instance, so I have to help her create space by moving us both away from the dog she feels afraid of. Giving Delta the agency to decide whether to interact with other dogs has helped her reactivity immensely, and she is now able to pass some dogs without reacting, providing there is space between them.

How Dogs Can Use Their Space – As we have just touched on, giving your dog the agency over how they use the space around them can help to reduce their stress levels. And, this can also be achieved inside your home by providing your dog with access to different areas of the house. Studies have shown that dogs in rescue kennels, that have access to an 'off-view' area tend to be less stressed than dogs who are shut into a 'full-view' area with no choice to remove themselves. This is also confirmed in studies of captive wild animals in zoos, who tend to show less behavioural issues and repetitive behaviours if they have the option to remove themselves to an area where visitors cannot see or interact with them. So, here is an example of how you can achieve this for your own dog at home:

- ***Undesirable option for your dog:*** *Being shut into the same room as your family & friends when they are at your house for a dinner party.*

- ***Slightly more desirable option for your dog, but still not one they would actively choose:*** Your dog is shut into a different room away from the party and any interaction from guests.
- ***Most desirable option for your dog:*** Providing them with a safe, comfortable place to retreat to, if this makes them feel more comfortable. Leave access to this place and let your dog decide if they would like to be involved or not!

Interactions With Adults – Not all dogs want to interact with all humans, and this is perfectly acceptable. However, all too often, dogs are still forced into situations where they feel uncomfortable around humans, where the humans are blissfully unaware of how they are making the dog feel. In fact, well-meaning dog lovers can be some of the worst offenders for this! Because they love dogs, they think that dogs will automatically love them because they are a 'doggy person,' so they bend over the dog and wave their hand in front of their nose to try and introduce themselves. However, this is not only quite rude in dog behaviour and body language terms, but it can also be overwhelming and scary for a dog to experience this. Here is what giving your dog agency in a situation like this could look like:

- ***Undesirable option for your dog:*** Allowing your guest to loom over your dog and wave their hand in their face.
- ***Slightly more desirable option for your dog, but still not one they would***

actively choose: Asking your guest to encourage your dog to take a treat from their hand. Your dog may still be uncomfortable about this, but may be pushed out of their comfort zone to access the treat.

- ***Most desirable option for your dog:*** Allowing your dog to approach the guest on their own terms, without direct eye contact or intimidating body language. Or, allowing your dog to safely retreat to a comfortable resting place without having to interact with the guest if this is what they would prefer to do.

Interactions With Children – This is another very common occurrence, whereby dogs are forced to interact with children of different ages, even though this makes them feel uncomfortable. Owners are often desperate to create a real-life fairy-tale where their dog and their child grow up together, are best friends, and life happily ever after. Unfortunately, though, this is not always in either side's best interests. There are thousands of videos circulating the internet that seem to show dogs and children living in harmony, however if you really study the body language of the dogs in question, they are often desperately unhappy with their situation. Here is how you could give your dog more agency over their interactions with children:

- ***Undesirable option for your dog:*** The child drapes all over the larger dog or picks up the smaller dog awkwardly. They may grab their fur, pull their ears, or poke them.

None of which is meant with malice by the child, but it is unpleasant for your dog.

- ***Slightly more desirable option for your dog, but still not one they would actively choose:*** The child is offering your dog a treat, meaning they still have to approach them to access a reward. This is still a somewhat forced interaction, although there is some benefit for the dog as a result.

- ***Most desirable option for your dog:*** Allowing your dog to freely remove themselves away from the child if this makes them feel more comfortable. Make sure if your dog chooses to do this, that you don't allow the child to follow them!

Interactions With Other Dogs – This is another commonly misunderstood and misinterpreted scenario for many dog owners. There is a mythical idea swirling around the canine world that all dogs should get on with every dog they meet. After all, they are all the same species, so they should get along just fine – right? Unfortunately, this is not always the reality. And, while many dogs do have plenty of canine companions, this is not always the way for others who would prefer to not interact with unknown dogs given the choice. And that is the key concept here, very few dogs have agency over meeting and interacting with other dogs, often because of their well-meaning owners think they should want to interact with members of their own kind. Here's an example:

You are walking with your dog, on a lead, down a footpath. An unknown dog approaches from the opposite way, heading in your direction, also on their lead.

- *Undesirable option for your dog:* Both dogs are forced to meet head on/face-to-face which is a very unnatural greeting method for dogs and can quickly lead to tension and confrontation.
- *Slightly more desirable option for your dog, but still not one they would actively choose:* Both dogs are forced to walk in close proximity to each other, without the chance of a calm greeting.
- *Most desirable option for your dog:* Create space between the two dogs, reduce tension on their leads, and only allow them to sniff each other briefly before moving on. Ideally, this should be nose to tail, which is a much more polite and natural way for dogs to greet each other. This should only be done if both dogs are actively seeking interaction with one another, their body language is relaxed and inquisitive, and the chances of the situation escalating into something negative, are low.

Consenting To Physical Touch – This is a slightly more complex category of agency, but giving your dog the control over whether they consent to being touched is something every owner should strive to do for them. If we think about this from a human perspective, it's a strange concept that we don't allow our dogs the same level of choice about what is done to their body. As humans, we are natural 'touchers.' We explore the world around us using our hands from a very early age, and our automatic reaction to seeing a dog is usually to try and stroke them. We love the feeling of their soft fur running through our fingers. We find comfort in stroking a dog's head. And, we enjoy ruffling up our dog's ears. However, not all humans stop to think about how this makes the dog feel. Do they genuinely enjoy it? And more importantly, would they choose for this to happen to them? The answer to these questions is not always.

For example, owners would often proclaim the following facts about their dog:

'She gets mean if people touch her when she is eating and will snap at them'
'He hates being restrained or held still'
'She doesn't like strangers approaching her'
'He gets scared if new people try to stroke him'
'She tries to bite if someone wakes her up from sleeping'
'He doesn't like being groomed/having his ears checked/having his teeth looked at/having his nails clipped etc'

Now, personally, I can relate to all of these findings, on a human level. In the same way that we might feel uncomfortable or uncertain if a stranger came up to us on the street and hugged us, or we might feel grumpy if we got suddenly woken up by someone shaking us, or we might have something mean to say if someone was constantly poking and irritating us when we were eating! All of the behaviours mentioned above are normal responses for the vast majority of dogs. Granted, some dogs will be seemingly okay with these things happening, although I doubt they would actively choose for any of them to happen if they had the option.

However, there are ways that you can provide your dog with agency over if they are happy to be physically touched. This comes in the form of co-operative care, which I wrote about in my previous book, 'Canine Contentment – The Essential Guide.' (You can find a sneak preview of the introduction from Canine Contentment at the end of this book.)

Co-operative care encourages your dog to let you know when they are comfortable to be physically touched, and when they are not. It acts as a form of communication between you and your dog which encourages you to respect their boundaries and gives your dog the choice to remove themselves from a situation they feel uncomfortable in. For example, it can be extremely useful to teach your dog a 'chin rest' whereby they rest their chin on an object like a table or chair, which is comfortable for them to do so. Then, provided they keep their chin resting on the table, they are consenting to you physically touching their paw in preparation for a nail trim for example. If at any point your dog lifts their chin from the table, this means they are uncomfortable and have then removed consent, meaning you should not continue to touch them.

Exercises like this aim to build up the trust your dog has in you. Every time you give your dog the choice to be touched, instead of just doing it anyway, this empowers them. It makes them feel more in control of their environment and their life, which is something many dogs often lack. This is the whole aim of giving your dog agency! Not only this, but I like to imagine it as depositing coins into a bank account. Each time you give your dog choices, it builds their trust in you, so more coins get added to their theoretical bank account. Then, in an emergency situation, where you may have to grab their paw to quickly remove a thorn, or apply ear drops for an infection, or bathe their eyes for example, this would withdraw some of the 'trust coins' from their bank account. If you are only ever withdrawing coins, and forcing your dog to do something that is scary and uncomfortable for them (even if it's in their best interest) then the coins will keep depleting which is not sustainable in the long run. This is easily avoided by preparing your dog and helping them feel more comfortable about these types of scenarios.

This type of training can also be widely seen in zoos. Teaching wild, captive animals how to willingly participate in certain activities reduces or even removes the need for any physical restraint or anaesthesia. Tigers are trained to open their mouth on cue, so their teeth can be examined. Sealions are taught to climb onto scales to monitor their weight. Gorillas are trained to sit still enough to have ultrasound scans done. Elephants can be taught to voluntarily offer their feet to have their nails checked. And these are just the tip of the co-operative care iceberg. So, this begs the question, if we can get wild animals, who have the potential to be extremely dangerous to humans, to not only tolerate these husbandry experiences, but voluntarily be participants of them, then why would we not do this for our dogs? Not only does co-operative care training have the potential to improve your dog's life, by making them feel more comfortable and in control, but it can also make your life easier too! You will no longer need to pin your dog down and force them to open their mouth to check their teeth, or wrestle with them to clip their nails. Less stress for them and less stress for you.

Does Agency Mean My Dog Can Do What They Want?

Yes and no! While agency does encourage your dog to have control over the environment and their actions, it's not always safe to let your dog do exactly what they really want to do all of the time. For example, if your dog loves to raid the bins, as much as they would want to choose to do this frequently, it could be detrimental to their health if they consumed something from the bin which was dangerous for them. And, in a scenario like this one, it's extremely unlikely that your dog would choose not to raid the bin, so it's up to you to manage the situation effectively, so they don't have the opportunity to put themselves at risk.

Or, your dog may prefer to fun freely off lead, but it wouldn't be appropriate for them to run across a busy road in the process. Agency is essential to your dog's wellbeing, but it should never be encouraged to the detriment of their health or safety. This is where enrichment and agency go hand in hand. If your dog wants to dig, and you provide them with a safely managed outlet for this behaviour in the form of a sandpit for digging in, this gives your dog agency.

Try to think of it like this. Instead of telling your dog 'you can never do this' you should aim to be saying 'I know that you need to do this, and you can do it here.'

But I Thought I Had To Be In Charge Of My Dog?

This is still a very common myth swirling around the dog world. Although, thankfully there is a wave of modern and positive dog ownership and training methods now, there are still trainers and owners following outdated trains of thought. The idea of us needing to show dominance over our dogs has now scientifically been debunked. In fact, even the scientists and researchers who originally came up with this idea, have since retracted their findings after more research was conducted. The original theory was based on studies of captive wolves, who did show dominance and submission to one another as part of their pack hierarchy. And so, because we know that dogs descended from wolves, it was assumed that they would likely behave in a similar way to them. However, the issue with the studies is that they focused on groups of unrelated, captive wolves which is far removed from how wolves would live and behave in the wild, making the findings inaccurate.

Wild wolves tend to live in family groups, and unlike the original research suggested, the leader of the group becomes so simply by breeding and producing offspring. These leaders are now usually referred to more accurately as the 'breeding female' and the 'breeding male' and not the 'alphas' as they once were. Captive wolves are often totally unrelated and are forced to interact and live alongside one another in relatively small enclosures. Again, this is a very unnatural way for a wolf to live. This adds a huge element of stress and unhappiness which is a more likely explanation for fights and displays of aggression being apparent in these scenarios. Not because this is how all wolves, or dogs, would naturally behave, which is where this misunderstanding originated from.

Frustratingly, humans have wrongly applied the idea of our domesticated dogs feeling the need to be part of a pack, and in turn, become the alpha of it, as factual. However, this couldn't be further from the truth. Our dogs do not view their family as their 'pack,' and they feel no need to rise through the ranks to become the leader of it either. In reality, our dogs are natural conflict-avoiders, choosing to always appease a situation in the first instance to try and avoid any potential conflict. They don't naturally want to start fights, or assert their dominance, quite the opposite in fact. This is always their last resort, when they have exhausted all other options and they feel like they have no other solution.

Put simply, our dogs are not on a mission to dominate, have power over, or control you or their environment. Their main aim isn't to be in charge or be the 'alpha,' or the 'top dog.' Therefore, there really is no need for you to become stuck in a power battle that doesn't need to exist whatsoever. In fact, many canine behaviour issues actually occur from a place of insecurity and the need to feel safe and secure. So, when you consider this, it seems wholly incorrect to approach your dog's training from a place of you trying to be dominant over them. This is the opposite of what your dog really needs in this instance, and that is a calm, committed, and supportive guardian who can help to guide them through life carefully and effectively. Force and aversive methods play no part in modern-day dog ownership, and they are certainly not ethical choices to opt for. After all, if we are encouraging our dogs to have more agency over their lives, do you really think they would choose to be shouted at, hit, shocked, chastised, dragged, and manhandled by their human? I highly doubt it!

Can My Training Methods Affect My Dog's Agency?

Yes, yes, and yes again! They absolutely can! As humans, we tend to stick with the notion that we are a superior species, and anything below us (including our dogs) should do as they are told and obey us. Stemming from this mindset is the desire to control our dogs, and force them into behaving as we want and expect them to, often with little to no consideration for what they truly need or desire. Thankfully, it is now widely understood and accepted that our dogs are sentient beings, capable of complex feelings and emotions. And so, with this in mind, if you choose to essentially bully your dog using fear, intimidation, and force to get them to behave a certain way, this removes any agency they have over their existence. This is a heart-breaking reality that some dogs still face each day, where they are not allowed to be who they are, or behave as they should, simply because it does not align with their owner's ideals.

However, thanks to an increased understanding of how effective positive training methods can be, a huge influx of dog owners actively want to become better guardians to their dogs. Fewer and fewer humans are battling to become the pack leader of their dog and instead opting for a kinder, more appreciative, and mutually beneficial existence for both themselves and their dogs. So, if you are one of these guardians, who genuinely wants to improve your dog's life by allowing them the freedom of choice, you are amongst friends here.

Shifting Your Mindset

Now, before we start on our enrichment journey, one more thing needs to be discussed before we dive in properly. *We need to change how we view our dog's behaviour.*

As we mentioned briefly in the introduction, lots of dogs display behaviours that humans don't like. Owners find their dog's behaviour problematic, irritating, and stressful.

But, fully understanding why your dog is behaving in a certain way can help you to figure out how is best to help them and in turn, reduce the frequency of them showing these undesirable behaviours.

So, instead of seeing your dog's behaviour as problematic, we need to accept that it's likely that our dogs are simply trying their best to navigate their way through our world. And, although they may not always get it 'right' in our eyes, they are only doing what they can to try and fit into our homes and lives. This is the biggest mindset shift you can have when it comes to knowing how to help your dog.

Perhaps your dog is digging up the garden, chewing your furniture, or howling when they are left. So, instead of automatically seeing this as a nuisance, really think about what the driving force is for them to behave in this way. Are they feeling bored or stressed? Are they looking for an outlet for their needs? Are they craving attention and thinking this is how they can access it quickly? There is always an emotion or feeling behind your dog's behaviour and they are not doing these things to give you a hard time.

All too often, we don't actively consider what our dog's needs truly are, and this is where behaviour problems can stem from. We often inadvertently force our dogs to fit into a certain mould, so they slot into our lives and don't cause us any trouble. We expect them to be quiet, well-behaved additions to our lives who never put a paw out of line.

However, if you put yourself into their place for a moment, it can help you understand how they are experiencing the world from their viewpoint. They are taken away from their siblings and mother and thrust into a strange new world where everyone and everything is new and strange. Everything smells different, there are new sounds, the people say things they don't understand, there may be other new dogs or animals they are now expected to be friends with. It is a lot to contend with for a pup who has probably only been alive for 8 weeks or so before all this happens to them.

And, it doesn't stop there. This strange new life continues as your pup grows into an adolescent, then an adult, and then a senior and all the extra hurdles these life stages bring. Your young dog has a desperate urge to explore the world by sniffing and chewing, but their human doesn't see the importance of this, so they pull them away from interesting smells and tell them they are naughty for chewing things.

Your adult dog has formed a strong bond with you and feels stressed when they are alone. They have all this pent-up energy, frustration, and stress and channel it into destroying your possessions to try and help themselves feel better, only for their human to shout at them and tell them it was wrong.

Your senior dog's joints ache and yet they are still forced to walk further, even though it causes them pain. They want to take their life at a slower pace, but are rushed through everything because their human's life is so busy.

So, I implore you to stop and think about what your dog truly needs in life. How can you meet their desires? How can you encourage them to show natural behaviours? How can you help them to live the best life possible? Shifting your mindset to prioritise your dog's individual needs instead of trying to make them fit around your own is perhaps the best thing you can do for your dog's well-being and happiness.

Accepting, appreciating, and encouraging your dog's natural behaviours, needs, and desires is a wonderful, ethical thing to do. And, this is where enrichment comes in! Adding this simple addition to your dog's life will instantly improve their happiness and the best news is, you can start today!

Now you are learning to see things from your dog's point of view and are starting to shift your way of thinking to be more in line with theirs, we are ready to dive into the wonderful world of enrichment!

Let's go!

What Is Enrichment & Why Is It Beneficial?

Enrichment is a real buzzword in the dog world now, but what does it actually mean? What is enrichment in relation to our dogs? Do our dogs really need it? What are the benefits? Is there more to it than playing games? What is the point of it all?

The first thing that often springs to mind when discussing enrichment activities for dogs are toys, games, and activities that in some way challenge them or give them something to think about. However, there is much more to enrichment than simply giving your dog something to do! There are whole other aspects to enrichment that are often overlooked because games and activities are usually prioritised.

The Oxford dictionary's definition of enrichment is; 'The action of improving or enhancing the quality or value of something.'

In the dog world, canine enrichment refers to enriching a dog's environment by encouraging them to use their senses and providing an outlet for them to display natural canine behaviours such as; chewing, licking, sniffing, digging, and chasing.

The idea of enrichment was first recognised in the 1920s. Scientists were studying chimpanzees in a laboratory setting and noted the benefits to their well-being when they were provided with interactive apparatus. Psychobiologist Robert Yerkes wrote about his findings and the benefits of enrichment opportunities for captive primates.

Then, from the 1950s onwards, zoologist Heini Hediger recognised the importance of enrichment for other captive animals kept in zoo settings. He was affectionately crowned the 'father of zoo biology' and researched extensively about how crucial enrichment was for these once-wild animals.

Fast-forward to the 1970s and along came Hal Markowitz, Animal Behaviour Professor at San Francisco State University. He has been regarded as one of the most influential researchers responsible for expanding our views and thoughts on the importance of enrichment. He focused closely on mimicking the natural behaviours of captive wild animals and using this as a form of beneficial enrichment. For example, teaching the animals how to search for and find their own food, solve problems, and make informed choices.

So, while our dogs are not technically captive wild animals, like the ones we find in zoos, they still lead somewhat 'captive' lives. They are not free to roam or hunt like their ancestors; they are governed by our human rules and standards. They look to us for food, water, shelter, healthcare, companionship, attention, interaction, and everything else they need to not only survive; but thrive too. We control when and what they eat, when and where they can relieve themselves, how much exercise they get, how much time they spend alone, how much interaction they get with their own kind, and every other aspect of their lives. When you realise just how much our dogs depend on us and how much say we have over their entire lives, it seems only fair that we allow them to behave like a dog as often as possible, too – right?

Over hundreds of years of domestication, it is true that our dog's natural 'wild' behaviours are more diluted than they would have been right at the start of their evolution. However, many of these natural, intrinsic behaviours are still very real and apparent. This is why enrichment activities are not just something that is done once or twice; it's essential they are factored into our dog's daily lives. The simple fact is, the more your dog is allowed to practice natural canine behaviours, the happier they will be.

Here's the benefits of canine enrichment:

Enrichment Provides An Outlet For Your Dog's Needs

Dogs that do not have a suitable outlet to channel their natural canine behaviours can be more likely to exhibit numerous behavioural issues including; unwanted chewing of furniture and possessions, digging up the garden or flooring in the home, separation anxiety, or excessive barking, for example. This is not done because your dog is intentionally being naughty, stubborn, or badly behaved.

These less-than-desirable behaviours are happening because your dog is trying their best to meet their needs and desires in the best way that they can, in the environment they find themselves in. Pair this with potentially heightened stress levels, an excessive amount of energy, and a build-up of frustration, and it's not hard to see why your dog may be behaving in this way. So, of course, it's not a long-term solution to let your dog raid the bins, destroy your home, and continue doing things that are likely to put them at risk. Instead, if your dog is behaving in this way, use it as an opportunity to recognise that their needs are not being met to a good enough standard and to change that.

The great news is that regular enrichment activities can help your dog to combat these feelings and provide them with an outlet for their intrinsic needs. Win, win!

Enrichment Can Build Your Dog's Confidence
Dogs who are generally nervous or uncertain can increase their confidence through enrichment activities. Setting them up for success and letting them 'win' by solving problems effectively increases their confidence. It also increases your dog's awareness of new and exciting things by introducing them in a safely managed way. i.e. new scents, textures, tastes, and sounds. To help increase your dog's confidence in enrichment activities, it's important that you start off with simple, easy-to-solve things so they stand a great chance of being

able to work out what to do quite quickly. If you start off with overly complex puzzles, or difficult games for a dog with low confidence, they will likely get frustrated, lose interest and not want to participate. This is exactly what we want to avoid, as this will decrease your dog's confidence even further which isn't something we want to intentionally do!

Enrichment Reduces Your Dog's Stress Levels

Because enrichment focuses on providing your dog with an outlet for their natural needs and desires, it's very relaxing for them to participate in. Unfortunately, whether intentional or not, our dogs often experience stress in their day-to-day lives. Although some dogs are better at processing this stress than others, some need more help and support in dealing with these feelings. Common things that can cause your dog some level of stress include; leaving them home alone, changes in their routine, living in a busy household, adding a new baby or pet to the family, not getting enough physical exercise, being fed a poor diet, illness or injury, stressful events (e.g. bonfire night), etc. Calming enrichment activities can help combat this stress and in turn, help your dog to feel more relaxed and happier.

Here are some examples of how enrichment can help to reduce your dog's stress levels:
Scenario: Your dog is sound sensitive, and nervous about loud, sudden, or new noises. You have family staying over at your home, including a young baby. When the baby cries, this is stressful for your dog

who has not experienced this before and so it unsettles them.

Solution: Ensure your dog has access to a safe, quiet space they can retreat to if they are feeling overwhelmed. This could be a crate with blankets over it, which can help muffle the noise somewhat. Play some calming music at a low volume in your dog's resting area to further reduce the sounds of the crying baby. Perhaps give them a long-lasting natural treat to chew on, as licking and chewing are natural stress-relievers for our dogs too.

Scenario: You have been working from home since you got your dog and now your job has changed which means you have to leave your dog home alone much more frequently than you have ever had to previously. Because your dog isn't really used to being left alone, this can make them feel stressed and anxious without your company.

Solution: Avoid high-intensity or repetitive exercise like chasing a ball as although this may tire your dog out physically, it leaves them feeling hyper and on an adrenaline high. This makes it much more difficult for them to settle down and relax and can increase the likelihood of them showing destructive behaviour in an attempt to calm themselves down. Pair this with the anxiety they are feeling by being home alone and it's not hard to understand why your dog may feel like they have to chew your shoes, or bark, or dig up the flooring!

Instead, try to take your dog for a Sniffari walk in the morning before you are due to leave for work. Sniffing is a natural, essential behaviour for our dogs and encouraging them to sniff is a stress-relieving exercise for them. This gives them chance to relieve themselves and catch up on all the new scents. Then, when you are back home, set up a snuffle mat for them to solve when you leave for work. Also make sure your dog has a comfortable resting place to relax in. Some owners find playing music beneficial as it helps reduce background noise from outside. If your dog barks at passers-by, try and manage their environment to reduce access to these triggers. I.e. close curtains/blinds, limit access to certain rooms using baby gates etc. A common mistake people make when trying to deal with their dog's separation anxiety is to only give their dog a snuffle mat before they leave their dog alone. This causes the snuffle mat to become a precursor to your dog being left, so as soon as they see it, they know what is about to happen which can increase their anxiety levels. Something we are trying to avoid! So, ensure to offer your dog a snuffle mat at different points, so they don't always associate it with being home alone.

Do you know the signs that your dog may be feeling stressed? Often, these signs can be subtle and therefore not immediately obvious until your dog's stress levels rise higher. If you can recognise the early warning signs of stress in your dog, you can help them to feel better faster. Here are some early indicators of stress in dogs: lip licking, yawning, avoiding eye contact, turning their head away, pacing, panting, drooling, shedding hair, self-mutilation (licking or chewing themselves excessively), body shakes (as if your dog is shaking off water), removing themselves from a situation, cowering, displacement behaviours (also known as fiddling around, so your dog could sniff the floor, lick themselves, etc instead of listening to cues) and appeasement gestures (like 'grinning', tip of the tail wagging, holding their body low to the ground, rolling onto their back to show their belly, etc.)

NOTE: While these are the generic signs of stress for some dogs, this is not the case for every individual dog. It's important to know your dog and their own personality and habits and what is normal behaviour for them. It's also essential to consider the context of the scenario too when looking for signs of stress. For example, if your dog has just been swimming and shakes themselves, this is purely to shake the excess water from their coat and not necessarily because they are stressed.

Or, if your dog loves to have their belly rubbed, they can roll over to show their belly as an invitation for you to pet it, not because they are stressed in that instance. But, if they are being growled at by another dog, and roll over to expose their belly, they are doing this to show the other dog that they are not a threat and to appease a stressful situation. Understanding what is normal for your dog, and looking at the circumstances they're in, can help you to better understand if your dog is stressed or not.

Enrichment Strengthens The Bond You Share With Your Dog
Not only does enrichment give your dog's brain a great deal of mental stimulation, but it can also

---

further strengthen the bond you share with each other. Treat enrichment as an adventure of finding out what new things you could try together today; this will really get your creativity flowing. This teamwork helps build trust between you and your dog and gives your dog more confidence in you. So, if they run into a difficult situation in the future, they can be more likely to come to you for help and support. If your dog is struggling to complete an enrichment activity, feel free to help and guide them. If they are finding it difficult to find the treats in a snuffle mat, try pointing them out for them. Or, if they are unsure about what to do when you give them a wrapped present, help them by starting to unwrap the present and encouraging them to do the same. This will increase your dog's trust in you, and they will enjoy sharing an enriching experience and natural behaviours with their human.

Enrichment Helps To Combat Over-Arousal
Arousal in canine behaviour terms refers to your dog being in a heightened emotional state. It means they are showing an intense reaction or emotion to something they are experiencing in their environment. Some dogs become over-aroused very quickly, which can be hard for owners to manage. And, if a dog spends a large portion of their life in a state of heightened arousal, this is not good for their long-term health and well-being. Different dogs can experience an increase in arousal levels for different reasons. Some may experience this when they see another dog and they become excited and frustrated because they want to go and greet them. Others can experience it when they are playing high-intensity,

repetitive games like fetch, because their adrenaline levels are raised. Generally speaking, a highly aroused dog will appear outwardly over-excited and may ignore any cues or requests from their owners. This can quickly get frustrating for owners who are left feeling like they have no control over their dog's behaviour. So, instead of trying to regain control and place limitations on your dog, you can provide them with an alternative outlet for these feelings by using enrichment. This can help your dog to calm down faster, and in turn, be in a better headspace for responding to your cues.

Enrichment Stimulates Your Dog's Olfactory System
Neophilia is the scientific term for a 'preference for novelty,' which helps explain why your dog will often take a keen interest in new scents. This is why they love to sniff every lamp post and blade of grass when you are out for a walk! Not only can your dog detect new scents that offer current information, but they can also detect historical information from scents which were left previously. Your dog can gather information like the health, age, sex, and even emotional state of another dog, just from sniffing a tiny droplet of their urine. Although it might seem gross to us, sniffing really is your dog's superpower! So much so, our dogs have approximately 300 million olfactory receptors in their nose, compared with humans who only have around 6 million. These olfactory receptors are responsible for collecting scent molecules, which are then processed by the olfactory bulb in your dog's brain, enabling them to understand what it is they

are smelling. The olfactory bulb in your dog's brain is almost 40 times larger than our human version. This shows exactly how important sniffing and scent are to your dog's life! Imagine having such a large part of your brain not being used to its full potential? This is what is happening to your dog when you deny them the opportunity to sniff!

This is why scentwork and the opportunity to sniff are so essential for your dog's well-being. Take a look at the chapter dedicated to dogs who love to sniff for some inspiration for activities to try. Your dog will thank you for it! The beauty of scent-based enrichment is that it is very easily accessible for dogs of any age, breed, size, or health status.

Enrichment Gives Your Dog's Brain A Workout

Enrichment activities get your dog's brain thinking, which is only ever a positive thing! It encourages your dog to solve problems and gives their brain a workout. This helps to combat boredom, relieve stress, and encourage cognitive function which is essential to long-term brain health and your dog's well-being. Our dogs are often left to their own devices for large portions of the day unless their owners are lucky enough to not have to go to work! But, this means that boredom can easily creep in, resulting in your dog looking for ways to entertain themselves. Boredom is where many potential behaviour issues stem from, so the sooner we can combat that by giving your dog's brain something to think about, the better!

Enrichment Encourages Your Dog To Do 'Dog Things'

Instead of constantly trying to prevent your dog from doing natural 'dog things,' enrichment actively encourages it! Although this may sound daunting, it is actually one of the best changes you can make to benefit your dog's life and your own. If you are constantly battling to try and control your dog's behaviour and make it more manageable, then enrichment activities can benefit you hugely. Listening, understanding, and providing what your dog truly needs is the biggest step to a happier life for both of you! With a little bit of creative thinking, you can even create a mutually beneficial arrangement that suits both you and your dog. For example, if your dog loves to dig, you can teach them to dig 'on cue' and then get them to help you with digging the borders in your garden. By cueing this digging behaviour this teaches your dog to 'help' you when you ask them to. This provides a suitable outlet for your dog's desire to dig and gets your jobs done faster in the process. You can also provide them with a sandpit where they are allowed to dig whenever they want to. And despite what some people may think, this won't encourage your dog to dig constantly anywhere, because their need to dig is being met in the areas you provide.

Enrichment Utilises The Natural Canine Predatory Sequence

Now, although this may sound a little bit scientific, it still applies to your dog, no matter what breed they are. Regardless of what they were bred to do, every dog naturally displays aspects of the predatory sequence. Our dog's wild ancestors relied upon the predatory sequence to find, catch, and kill prey which they ate to survive. And, although our dogs no longer need to do this so they can eat, they still retain certain parts of this natural predatory sequence. It looks a little something like this:

Orient > Eye > Stalk > Chase > Grab-Bite > Kill-Bite > Dissect > Consume

The vast majority of dogs no longer display this sequence in full, and some breeds naturally prioritise different aspects of this sequence.

For example, my Border Collies, and other herding breeds, concentrate on the *Orient > Eye > Stalk > Chase* part of the sequence, as this is what a shepherd would need them to do to round up livestock successfully. Terriers would concentrate on the *Chase > Grab-Bite > Kill-Bite* aspects of the sequence which is what makes them excellent at catching and killing rodents for pest control. And, although most domesticated dogs no longer need to carry out the dissection and consumption parts of this sequence in order to survive, it is still a natural behaviour which is deeply ingrained for them, and these aspects are something they would still likely enjoy today. This is why many dogs enjoy shredding activities like ripping open a wrapped present to access treats inside. This replicates the dissection and consumption part of the predatory sequence.

Recognising and understanding which parts of the predatory sequence apply to your dog, can help you to decide which enrichment activities would be best suited to them.

Enrichment Makes Your Dog's Life Better
Enrichment adds excitement and interest to your dog's daily life. Allowing and encouraging our dogs to practice natural behaviours regularly, releases feel-good hormones known as endorphins, which help them to feel happier, relaxed, and contented. This is exactly what we want to achieve! Enrichment shouldn't be something you do every so often; it should ideally become part of your dog's daily life. Providing an outlet for their intrinsic needs and desires and allowing them to practice these natural canine behaviours is a sure fire way to improve your dog's life!

Enrichment Can Improve Your Life Too!
Although it may sound strange that providing your dog with enrichment opportunities has the potential to improve your life too, it is absolutely true! Because you are providing your dog with suitable outlets for their natural needs and desires, enrichment has the potential of reducing behaviour issues from occurring. So, instead of your dog chewing up your furniture, damaging your possessions, or developing other behaviours you may see as a nuisance, they will be able to channel this into something productive and interesting for them. This can make your life easier because your dog is happier and not intent on destroying your home and belongings. So, this means enrichment can easily improve your life too, not just your dog's.

Which Dogs Can Benefit From Enrichment?

The simple answer to this is ANY dog can benefit from enrichment! The beauty of enrichment is that there are aspects of it that can benefit any dog, no matter what their age, breed, background, prior learning experience, training level, personality, or individual needs are. You don't need to dedicate a lot of time, money, or resources to enrichment activities, which is what makes it so appealing and accessible to dog lovers around the world.

Young Puppies
Enrichment can be started at any age; in fact, the earlier you start, the better! Try to look at enrichment as something you can factor into your puppy's daily life and then continue throughout their entire life. Young puppies can benefit from certain enrichment activities even before they have left their littermates and mother. The more opportunities your pup has to practice enriching activities, the better! Responsible, educated breeders will introduce their puppies to basic enrichment activities to help them explore their environment and build their confidence. Here are some examples:
- Toys that move, make different sounds, or emit lights.
- Providing different textures for pups to play on like; artificial grass, carpet, rubber mats, grass, wood flooring, etc.

- Using different ways of feeding puppies when they are weaned like; lickmats, bowls made of varied materials, providing natural chews etc.
- Offer obstacles that move like; wobble boards, pillows, large plastic bottles, etc to encourage the pup's awareness of their body and surroundings.
- Introduce household sounds like; washing machines, TVs, radios, ovens, microwaves, alarm clocks, hoovers, etc so the pups are not startled by these noises when they come home with you.
- Early socialisation with new people, other pets and other dogs before the puppies are sent to their new homes can help them become more confident with future introductions.
- The breeder's aim should be to teach their puppies that the world is an exciting place to explore, not something that should be feared.

Enrichment is essential for your puppy's development and for building their confidence. A process known as 'habituation' is how your pup gets used to interacting with things both inside and outside. Without this, your puppy can feel anxious in new situations and be unsure about interacting with new things.

For example, if your puppy has never walked on different textured surfaces before, they are more likely to be wary of doing so as they grow. Successful habituation helps to expand your puppy's horizons and encourages them to feel more confident in their own abilities. Habituation is a process that should be continued through your puppy's life and throughout their adulthood too.

The saying of 'if you don't use it, you lose it' applies to habituation as for example, even if puppies are encouraged to walk on different surfaces when they are young, and they have a prolonged break where they don't do this, they may feel wary once more when they are required to do this again.

Adult Dogs
Healthy adult dogs of any breed will enjoy all kinds of different enrichment activities! Not only will this help to keep their mental health in good shape, but it can also help to keep their body fit, increase their confidence, and strengthen the bond that you share with each other too. Start off by considering your dog's breed, personality, and preferences to find out what type of enrichment they might like to try out. We shall look at this in more detail in the chapters ahead.

Senior Dogs
Some older dogs may be more limited with the amount and type of physical exercise they can participate in. However, this is where enrichment activities can really benefit them! Just because their body may not allow them to do everything they used to, doesn't mean that their mind isn't still craving something to get them thinking. You can tailor the type of enrichment activities you offer to your senior

dog, to make sure they suit their abilities. Choosing slower, calming, gentle activities for your elderly dog will help keep them physically active, give their brain a workout, and reduce the risk of them over-exerting themselves through too much physical exercise. Some studies have shown that regular enrichment activities can help slow down or prevent canine cognitive decline, meaning your dog's brain can stay sharper for longer. Canine Cognitive Dysfunction (CCD) is a relatively common condition found in older dogs, which is similar to Dementia in humans. Research suggests that providing your senior dog with plenty of enrichment opportunities can help to reduce the speed of which CCD affects their brain.

Older dogs are often side-lined for certain activities simply because of their age, but the beauty of enrichment is that you can tailor your activity to suit their individual needs. So, there is no reason to leave the old dogs behind! The idea that old dogs can't learn new tricks isn't strictly true either. So, even if your dog has never tried a particular activity before and they are already a senior, there is no reason why they can't learn how to do it. Granted, it may take more repetitions for your dog to get the hang of it, compared with a younger dog, but if you are patient, understanding, and consistent, there is nothing your old dog can't learn!

Any Breed Of Dog
No matter what breed your dog is, there are enrichment activities to suit them. There is often a misconception that your dog needs to be of a high

intelligence level to get the most out of enrichment. However, this couldn't be further from the truth! Granted, if your dog is naturally brainy, then they will have an advantage when it comes to activities that involve problem-solving and thinking. But this is not essential by any means! Enrichment is empowering for your dog and as we have previously mentioned, it helps to increase their confidence too. So, even if your dog is shy, or withdrawn, you may be surprised just how intelligent they are when they start to feel more confident and empowered. Different breeds will naturally have various strengths too, which can help you to decide which enrichment activity to choose. For example, Hounds tend to excel at sniffing, Herders love to chase, Terriers love to shred, etc. We shall look at how your dog's breed can affect the type of the enrichment activity they prefer, later on.

Dogs From Any Background
It doesn't matter if you have had your dog from a breeder, or rescue centre, or what their background and experiences have been so far. You can tailor their enrichment activities to suit them best. Your dog doesn't have to be trained to a high level, either. Enrichment is accessible to all dogs, no matter what! Whether your dog comes from a line of championship-winning obedience dogs, or they're a mixed breed rescue whose history is unknown, it makes no difference. Enrichment can be equally beneficial to any dog, despite their background, genetics, or experience. There are no prerequisites that your dog needs to be able to benefit from enrichment.

High Energy Dogs

Dogs that are considered as 'working breeds' tend to be high-energy. This means that not only do they require higher amounts of physical exercise than more sedate dogs, but they also need more mental stimulation too. A common mistake owners often make is continually increasing their dog's physical exercise more and more. However, no amount of physical exercise, even to the point of exhaustion, will fully satisfy the needs of your dog. This is where enrichment activities are crucial! Not only do they give your active dog's brain a workout, but they also give them a chance to relax, unwind, and calm down which can be beneficial after exercise. A combination of physical exercise and enrichment activities is the key to a happy, balanced dog!

Nervous Or Anxious Dogs

Enrichment can be excellent for building confidence in dogs who are anxious or nervous. There are lots of different exercises and activities that encourage your dog to explore and problem-solve. If you set them up so your dog can be successful, it will increase their confidence and make it more likely for them to attempt it more readily in the future.

Plus, if their anxiety can make 'normal' walks more difficult or stressful for your dog, enrichment activities can be done at home where they feel more comfortable. Once they feel more confident, enrichment can be practised more in the outside world too.

If your dog struggles to settle down properly at home, and paces, whines, and pants, then enrichment can go some way to helping them calm down. Calming enrichment activities release feel-good hormones into your dog's system, which naturally helps them settle down and unwind. Choosing activities that encourage sniffing, licking, chewing, and relaxation, can go a long way towards calming a nervous dog and helping to improve their confidence, so they don't feel as anxious in the future.

Dogs With Different Personalities & Preferences

If your dog is naturally confident and outgoing – great! If they are more reserved and shy – no problem! If your dog enjoys the company of other dogs or prefers not to be around them – either will work. Foodie dogs, sniffy dogs, diggy dogs, barky dogs, and any other kind of dog will find enrichment beneficial! We will look in more detail in the chapter's ahead at the types of enrichment your own dog may find most interesting and enjoyable. An activity that one dog loves, may be boring or too easy for another dog, but the great news is, there is something for everyone. Enrichment is very inclusive!

Dogs With Additional Needs

If your dog is deaf or blind, or even uses a doggy wheelchair, there are still plenty of enrichment activities they will love to take part in! So, while they may not be able to participate in everything we will look at in this book, the beauty of enrichment is that you can tailor it to suit the needs of any dog, no matter what additional needs you have to consider. Deaf or blind dogs can still be shown how to use a snuffle mat, or taught tricks, or shred presents, or dig in a sandpit for example, in the same way that a hearing dog would! You would simply have to adjust your positive training methods to suit their individual needs. I.e. use a thumbs up gesture to your deaf dog to indicate they are doing the right thing, before rewarding them with a treat and/or physical praise. Or, gently direct your blind dog or lure them with treats to encourage them to access different textured surfaces, or use a toy that crinkles or squeaks as they play with it. Dogs in wheelchairs can also easily use a snuffle mat, go on sniffaris, learn their toys by name, or be taught to speak on cue.

Dogs Who Are Recovering From Injury Or Illness

Enrichment can also be beneficial for dogs whose physical exercise amounts need to be reduced, whether that is temporarily or long-term. For example, following surgery or when recovering from an injury. The thought of not physically exercising a dog would fill many with utter dread; however, using a combination of enrichment techniques and activities can relieve the stress from both you and your dog!

Your dog would understandably have raised stress levels following surgery or during periods of recovery, as they will most probably have a change in routine (not going for walks when they usually would or staying on a lead when they are usually let off lead), but it is also likely that they will have some level of pain present too. They may also have to contend with wearing protective equipment, such as a plastic cone collar, an inflatable collar, a body suit, a bandage, or a cast, to stop them from being able to interfere with their wound until it is fully healed. The combination of all of these factors is undoubtedly going to increase their stress levels, which is why enrichment activities during periods of convalescence are so helpful.

How Do I Use Enrichment?

The aim of enrichment is to improve your dog's mental well-being, and in turn, their life as a whole. But how often should you be providing enrichment activities for your dog? And how difficult should these activities be for them? We will look at how you can get the most out of enrichment in this chapter:

How Do I Introduce Enrichment If My Dog's Never Done It Before?

The first rule is to start off simple and only increase the difficulty gradually over time! Be prepared to help your dog to figure out what to do, and reward them heavily for doing the right thing. This will encourage them to try new things and will increase their trust in you because you have helped them with something they were struggling with. Keep your sessions short, positive, upbeat and encouraging to keep your dog engaged and interested in your chosen activity.

How Often Should I Provide Enrichment Activities?

Ideally, you should aim to provide your dog with enriching activities every day! This may sound daunting, but as we will explore throughout this book, it is much easier to implement this than you may think. The more chances your dog has to show natural canine behaviours, exercise their brain, move their body, and relax and unwind, the better.

How Long Should Each Enrichment Session Last?

A common misconception for enrichment is that each activity should keep your dog busy for as long as possible. However, if this is the case, it's likely your dog will end up feeling frustrated or become bored of the activity. The length of each session will vary between dogs and for different activities too. For example, a dog may enjoy a snuffle mat for 10 minutes, but is happy to chew on a natural treat for 20 minutes. So, there isn't really a hard, set rule for the length of time your session should last for. The main thing to remember is that you want to avoid your dog becoming frustrated, bored, or very tired, because this will make them lose interest in the enrichment opportunity. This is exactly the opposite of what we want to achieve. We want to help our dogs to feel relaxed, settled, and secure. Positive emotions and feelings all the way!

Should I Make The Exercises More Difficult?

Only increase the difficulty of your problem-solving enrichment activities if your dog finds them exceptionally easy. If you start off at a high level of difficulty, your dog will get frustrated and lose interest in the activity very quickly. This is the exact opposite of what we are aiming for when we provide enriching opportunities for our dogs, we want to be adding something positive, not negative. Starting off at an easier level helps to increase your dog's confidence and will set them up for success when they encounter something a little trickier next time.

What Treats Should I Use For Enrichment Activities?

Not all enrichment activities involve food or treats, but they are a crucial element for some exercises. The treats you use should be easy for your dog to eat, meaning they should be small enough for them to not need to chew them up too much. Higher-value treats tend to be ideal so things like; cooked chicken, cheese, sausages, liver, cheese spread, meat paste, etc. You can also use your dog's own dry food if they are kibble fed, or their wet food for spreading onto lick mats or Kongs for example.

Care must be taken to not let your dog become overweight, so it's important to keep an eye on the amount of food they are consuming. Treats should only make up the minority share of your dog's daily food allowance, especially the higher-value treats mentioned above as they can contain higher amounts of fat. Try to avoid shop-bought processed treats if possible as they often contain artificial colours, flavours, and preservatives which your dog doesn't benefit from. Sticking to natural treats is best if this is possible, though the odd bit of 'junk' food like a teeny bit of grated cheese in a snuffle mat shouldn't do any harm.

Set Your Dog Up For Success

This is one of my life's mottos for all aspects of dog training, but it applies to enrichment too! If you make the activity so hard that your dog can't succeed, they will lose interest and will give up trying to solve it. They will soon recognise that this is not worth their energy trying to figure out. So, set them up for success whenever possible. You are best keeping your enrichment activities really easy for your dog to 'win' at first to help build their confidence. Once they have got the hang of it, then you can increase the difficulty, but if there is any sign of frustration, take a break and choose an easier activity instead.

Our dogs, just like us, have their own strengths, weaknesses, and preferences. So, what one dog may excel at, may be really difficult for another dog. And something that one dog loves and looks forward to, may be another dog's worst nightmare! So always keep this in mind. Enrichment is a learning journey to help you discover what your dog enjoys the most and what helps them to be happiest!

Work Together With Your Dog
Enrichment is a two-way street! Yes, the aim is to improve your dog's life, happiness, and well-being but they rely on you to provide them with these opportunities. All too often, enrichment is seen solely as something to just keep your dog busy, but it is also an opportunity for you to improve the relationship with your dog through teamwork too. If your dog has never done a certain activity before, they may well need a helping hand from you to point them in the right direction. So, feel free to give them a clue and work together to get the job done! This will help your dog to build their confidence and increase the likelihood of approaching new tasks positively in the future. It will also help them feel more confident knowing that you are in their corner, working with them to help them feel better, instead

of you trying to stop them from doing certain things or behaving in a certain way.

How Do I Know Which Enrichment Activity To Choose?

Different breeds of dogs naturally have different traits, characteristics, and preferences. This is why we love them so much because they are all so unique! So, when you are thinking of which enrichment activities may be best suited to your dog, a good place to start is considering your dog's breed and what they were actually bred to do. For certain dog breeds, it's widely known and understood what their intended purpose is. I.e., Border Collies are used for herding livestock, Labradors are used as gundogs, etc. However, even the lovely little lap dogs we know, and love today, once had a specific purpose in life.

For example, there is a current trend for Dachshunds; they are everywhere! These sweet little sausage dogs are everyone's favourite, but how many people actually know what they were originally bred for? In reality, these cute-looking long dogs were bred for hunting. They're required to scent, track, chase, and flush out burrowing animals like badgers and rabbits. They then bark when they are underground to scare the prey out of hiding and alert the hunter to their whereabouts so they can be dug out of the ground. So, this means they are likely to be barkers, diggers, and chasers. Some of these traits are never considered when you look at a Dachshund snuggling up on the sofa, but they are still there.

If you are unaware of these traits, or simply choose to ignore them, then this is when the behaviour problems can start to materialise. If you combine a dog who is very bonded with their owner, who is left alone while you go to work, with one that is a master at digging, you will soon find holes in your flooring or scratches at your door. This is not your Dachshund being naughty, it is simply them expressing their natural breed traits to try and combat the stress they are feeling. They do this because these natural traits are easy for them to practice and make them feel better.

So, when considering which type of enrichment activity your dog might like; think of your dog's breed. And, if you don't know already what they were originally bred for, then research it! If you have a crossbreed, research all the breeds that make up your dog so that you have a clear idea of what their natural breed traits are likely to be.

Over thousands of years of selective breeding, each individual dog breed has been carefully curated into something useful for humans. We have bred Terriers for pest control, Shepherds for guarding and herding livestock, Gundogs for hunting, Toy breeds for companionship, and many more. And, even if the Labrador you add to your family isn't going to be used for retrieving game, this doesn't mean that these natural skills that have been carefully bred into your canine companion have gone away. They are still there, it's still something they want to do desperately, and they will find a way to practice these feel-good behaviours in the best way they can. Even if that means that the only thing that they will be retrieving from now on, is your slippers!

If dogs with such strong breed traits do not have a way to channel them appropriately then this can be a recipe for disaster. A favourite phrase of mine is 'If you do not give your dog a job to do, then they will go self-employed and you may not like the job they choose' For example, a Border Collie may chase cars or bikes and a Dachshund may dig up the garden! It is an unrealistic expectation for our dogs to simply 'set aside' these intrinsic needs just for our own human convenience.

In fact, many dogs are no longer required to carry out the 'jobs' they have been bred for centuries for. It's much more common to see Labradors lazing on someone's sofa, than out on a shoot retrieving game. But as we already know, these needs, desires, and skills don't simply go away if our dogs are not actively using them. So, it's our job to fill in these gaps so our dogs are still leading fulfilling lives.

So, now you have a better understanding of what your dog's breed was intended for, this can help you decide on the most suitable form of enrichment for them. Next, we will look at a whole host of different activities, designed to be engaging, interesting, and of course, enriching for your dog.

Get ready for some fantastic enrichment ideas for your dog to enjoy!

Enrichment Ideas For Dogs Who Love To Chase

Lots of dogs LOVE to chase! It's a natural part of the canine predatory sequence. No matter which part of the predatory sequence has been encouraged through breeding, pretty much all dog breeds want to carry out the chasing aspect. Chasing leaves your dog on an adrenaline high, which is what makes it so enjoyable and addictive for them. Because it makes them feel good, they want to do it more and more!

So, if you don't provide an outlet for this strong desire to chase, this is when dogs can start to chase things you would rather they didn't, like wild animals, other dogs, cats, small pets, etc. The ideas listed below can help to provide your dog with a safe way to exercise their chasing desires in a safely managed way.

NOTE: Because the chase is one of the earlier stages of the predatory sequence, it can become frustrating for your dog if they just repeatedly play chasing games, without the chance to progress through the sequence further. So, it's a good idea to follow these games up with some ideas from the 'Enrichment Ideas For Dogs Who Love To Play' and 'Enrichment Ideas For Dogs Who Love To Shred' chapters which encourage the grab-bite, dissection and consumption aspects of the predatory sequence.

This will help your dog to feel more fulfilled, as they have successfully completed the sequence.

Flirt Poles – Ideal for: Impulse control, physical exercise & chasing

Flirt poles can be made yourself or purchased ready-made. They are essentially a toy attached to a bungee line, which is attached to a solid pole. You then hold the pole and 'flirt' the toy around (hence the name!) and encourage your dog to chase it. Flirt poles are great for enrichment and are sure to be a hit if your dog loves to chase and grab things. They are also good for encouraging impulse control by allowing your dog to see and stalk the toy, without instantly trying to grab it straight away. Some people think of them as cat wands for dogs as the basic principle is the same!

Lure Games – Ideal for: Impulse Control, physical exercise & chasing

Lure games work in a similar way to the flirt pole in that you drag a toy or 'lure' across the ground for your dog to chase. This is particularly popular for terriers, hounds and other breeds traditionally used for hunting. Lure games encourage your dog to eye, stalk and chase the lure, which mimics the natural canine predatory sequence.

Fetch – Ideal for: Physical exercise & chasing

Fetch might sound a little bit basic, but most dogs love to play it! In fact, even for breeds that are not naturally drawn to fetching and retrieving, it can still be a great enrichment activity. Teaching your dog to chase, catch and retrieve a toy offers both a brain and body workout.

NOTE: High-energy and working breeds can be especially prone to becoming obsessed or addicted to the thrill of fetching a toy, so this should only be played in moderation and never to the point of exhaustion. For dogs who become obsessed with chasing a ball or playing fetch, it's essential to teach them a 'finished' cue to let them know that the game is over and it's time to stop. Because fetch repeats the same parts of the predatory sequence (chase and grab-bite) over and over again, this can become frustrating for your dog because they can never progress to the next parts of the predatory sequence. It also has high impact on your dog's joints and muscles which can lead to injuries or long-term issues. So, once you have let your dog play fetch for a little while, it's a good idea to replicate the next part of the predatory sequence (dissection and consumption) by allowing your dog to shred up their toy or eat some treats from the ground. Toys that you can hide food in can be an excellent choice for this type of game, as your dog can 'shred' them to access the treats, without actually damaging the toy beyond repair.

You can also add another element to your fetch game which increases the difficulty. Here's how to do it:

Step 1 – Ask your dog to sit and wait (or get a helper to hold them) while you throw the ball/toy.
Step 2 – Wait for the ball/toy to land on the ground then release your dog and ask them to 'find it.'
Step 3 – Help your dog by pointing to where the ball/toy is if they need some extra help.
Step 4 – Praise them for finding the ball/toy and repeat the game.

This also reduces the risk of your dog jumping up to catch the ball/toy from the air which can increase the chances of them landing awkwardly and potentially injuring themselves. It still maintains the chase element that your dog loves, without the high impact of jumping up or stopping suddenly to grab the ball/toy.

Herding Ball – Ideal for: Chasing, physical exercise & outlet for natural instincts

Ideal for the dog breeds that are bred for herding, but other breeds can enjoy this too! Herding balls are essentially large-sized, tough, plastic balls that are too large for your dog to pick up and they are designed to be pushed around by your dog. This mimics the chasing and rounding up aspect of herding, which Shepherds, Border Collies, Heelers, and other herders crave!

Although most dogs would be happy to whizz around the garden or park with their herding ball, there is an official dog sport which replicates this known as Treibball (pronounced Tri-Ball). This sport already has quite a large following in the USA, but the UK is catching up with the benefits of it now too, with some dog clubs across the country now offering classes. The aim of Treibball is to teach your dog to do an 'outrun' where they run towards the group of herding balls. Once they get there, they need to push the herding ball back to into a goal, a bit like herding sheep into a pen. This is why the herding breeds especially excel at this activity, but it is open to any breed to give it a go.

Frisbee – Ideal for: Chasing & physical exercise

Frisbee works on the same basis as fetch, but instead of fetching a ball or other toy, your dog is fetching a frisbee. The benefit of this is that a frisbee tends to stay airborne for longer than other toys, which adds interest for your dog. However, it's best to avoid the cheaper plastic frisbees, as these can easily snap and splinter into sharp shards when your dog grabs them. So, it's best to use frisbees designed specifically for dogs. Care should also be taken to discourage your dog from grabbing the frisbee while it's high up in the air, as this can cause them to land awkwardly and risk potential injury.

Chasing You – Ideal for: Chasing, impulse control & bond-building

For this game, you can turn yourself into part of the fun! This can be easier to do if you have a helper, but you can do it on your own if your dog has a reliable 'wait' cue. The aim is to get your dog to wait (or your helper to hold them) while you run ahead to create some distance between you. While you are still moving, call your dog and get them to run full speed towards you! When they get to you, reward them with a game of tug-of-war or a delicious treat. It's best to stay in the eyesight of your dog so they don't start panicking if they can't see you.

Bubbles – Ideal for: Chasing & grabbing

Make sure the bubbles you choose are dog-friendly ones, you can even get flavoured bubbles like bacon, or peanut butter to make them even more interesting for your dog. Blow the bubbles outside and encourage your dog to chase and pop them. This exercise can become frustrating for some dogs though, as they never have anything to 'show' for their chase. The natural predatory sequence for dogs includes the chase, then a grab bite, then a kill bite, then dissection, and then consumption. This game concentrates solely on the chase and grab aspects, so it's good to do some calmer activities as a follow-up.

Treat Bowling – Ideal for: Chasing & physical exercise

Treat bowling is as easy as it sounds! Simply call your dog and bowl a treat in the opposite direction (behind you). Then encourage your dog to chase it and find their reward. Not only is this an enrichment activity, but it can also help to improve your dog's recall. The aim is to encourage them to run at full speed back to you, in anticipation of chasing a treat you have bowled across the ground for them. You can even give this game a cue like 'bowl,' so your dog knows what is about to happen.

Enrichment Ideas For Dogs Who Love To Sniff

Sniffing is one of the most universally necessary behaviours for dogs to display, regardless of their breed or age. As we have already mentioned, our dog's superpower is sniffing, and it really is essential that they are allowed to practice this as often as possible. Sniffing is also one of the easiest and most accessible enrichment activities that you can implement in your dog's life.

Processing scents is actually quite tiring for your dog, and although it's not intended as a total replacement for physical exercise, they do work in synergy with each other. And, because every single breed of dog naturally wants to sniff (and enjoys it!) there are so many different options for them to enjoy.

Snuffle Mats – Ideal for: Sniffing & foraging

Snuffle mats have gained huge popularity over recent years. These are most commonly backed with rubber matting to avoid the mat slipping, and fleece or other material is then threaded through the mat to create interesting textures. Food can then be scattered and hidden within the fabric, and your dog is encouraged to snuffle and sniff out the treats. These are an example of a 'foraging' toy which encourages your dog to utilise their intricate sense of smell which is one of the most crucial natural behaviours they need to have a chance to exhibit regularly.

Thousands of 'snuffle products' are available to purchase now because they have grown so much in popularity in recent years. A whole array of different mats are available, each with assorted designs and levels of difficulty depending on your dog's needs. There are also snuffle balls, snuffle snakes, snuffle cubes and many more! The possibilities are endless. And if that wasn't enough, there is of course the option of you making your own versions too!

Sniffaris – Ideal for: Sniffing & mental stimulation

The affectionate term for walks where your dog has plenty of opportunies to sniff! Sniffing is a fundamentally natural behaviour for all dogs, but some breeds enjoy it even more than most. Take your dog to areas where you know there will be lots of new scents for them to delve into. Places, where there have been lots of other dogs, people, or wildlife, are ideal choices for your Sniffari.

No rushing, pulling your dog away, or moving on before your dog is ready! Remember, scent is the way in which your dog interacts with the world around them. It's like their own doggy version of social media. It's only fair to your dog to let them catch up on what's going on around them in the world, just like we do!

Let Your Dog Lead – Ideal for: Sniffing, mental stimulation & confidence building

The next step up from a Sniffari, where you choose the route, is to let your dog decide which direction they want to go. There is often a big focus on walking your dog for a certain length of time or taking them on a certain route. but have you ever stopped to think about where your dog would choose to walk? Letting your dog choose the route you take is enriching and empowering for them. And, it adds interest to their day and yours by changing up the usual routine.

Natural Snuffle Mats – Ideal for: Sniffing & foraging

If you have a lawn at home, consider leaving part of it longer next time you mow it. And voila! You have an instant, natural snuffle mat, which is great for throwing treats in. It will take your dog longer to sniff out and find the treats in the long grass than it would on a short lawn or hard ground. You could also replicate this by growing long grass in a plant pot or container to achieve the same result if you don't have a lawned garden. Make sure to avoid using any chemicals like weed killers, or growth enhancers in your garden if your dog has access to it, as many of them are not pet-safe. So, the last thing we would want is your dog sniffing something which could be dangerous to their health.

If you are out on a walk, take a look at the environment you are walking in and see if there are any other areas that are safe for your dog to use as a natural snuffle mat. Examples could be; patches of long grass in a field, in a woodland amongst some pinecones or fallen leaves, or amongst some pebbles on a stony beach.

NOTE: Only utilise natural snuffle mats if you are certain that your dog won't eat the substances (stones/leaves/etc.) that you are hiding your treats amongst.

Hide & Seek (Treats/Toys) – Ideal for: Sniffing, mental stimulation & seeking

Once your dog is used to sniffing out treats or toys, you can increase the difficulty by hiding them in trickier places. Cardboard boxes and other containers are great for this! This can be done around your home, garden, or out on walks. Consider different heights and textures when deciding where to hide your treats or toys. So, put some on the sofa, under the footstool, under a pillow, on a log, behind a door, under a blanket, on the dog bed, etc. anywhere you can think of that your dog will be able to find. If they are finding it difficult, you can help them by pointing to the right place and encouraging them to investigate. This will build the relationship you share with your dog as well as increase their trust in you to help them out when they need it.

Treat Logs – Ideal for: Sniffing & foraging

Time for a bit of DIY! Ideally, choose a log that is too big for your dog to pick up. Next, drill some holes into it that are big enough to fit some tasty treats in. Then, place it outside filled with delicious treats and encourage your dog to sniff them out. This could also be fastened to a fence or propped up securely so that your dog has to reach up and put their front feet onto the log to reach the treats. You could also replicate this when you are out on walks, by taking some spreadable treats such as cream cheese, pate, or meat paste out with you and smearing some onto the trunk of a tree or large rocks. Again, you can encourage your dog to reach up and lick the treats from the tree or rock.

Pick A Hand – Ideal for: Sniffing & mental stimulation

This is quite a straightforward game to teach your dog and something that can be done anywhere. Here's how you teach it:

Step 1 – Hold a treat in the palm of your hand and close it to make a fist.
Step 2 – Make a fist with your other hand (without a treat in!)
Step 3 – Hold out both hands in front of you for your dog to sniff.
Step 4 – If they sniff the hand that contains the treat, open up your hand to let them eat it. (If they continually sniff the empty hand, you can open it up to show them there is nothing inside, then when

they sniff the other hand, reward them with the treat)
Step 5 – Your dog will quickly get the hang of choosing the correct hand and you can practice this anywhere! The more places you can do it the better.

Cups Game – Ideal for: Sniffing & mental stimulation

This game is similar to the 'pick a hand game' but instead of using your hands, you use plastic cups on the ground. Here's how to play:

Step 1 – Place a treat on the floor and cover it with a plastic cup.
Step 2 – Place a second plastic cup on the floor next to the first (without a treat in!)
Step 3 – Let your dog sniff them and they should knock over the cup with the treat underneath so they can eat it.

NOTE: If you want to make this a little harder, don't let your dog see which cup you have put the treat underneath! You can also add more empty cups so it's not as obvious to them which is the correct one.

Hanging Cups Game – Ideal for: Sniffing & mental stimulation

This follows the same principle as the 'cups game' but this time, instead of the cups being placed on the floor, you thread them through a string and tie them up. Treats can be placed in the cups, and you can

encourage your dog to sniff and paw at the cups to knock the treats out of them.
Tie the string of cups at a suitable height for your dog so they can access the treats without stretching too high or getting frustrated.

Scentwork – Ideal for: Sniffing & mental stimulation

There are more and more dog training classes aimed specifically at scentwork popping up across the country, it is much more commonplace now than it was just a few years ago. This is because the benefits of it are becoming more widely known and understood! Some classes offer scentwork just for fun, whereas others go on to compete in trials, so choose whichever is best for you and your dog. The aim is similar to that of official working detection dogs (search & rescue, explosives, customs, etc), but for our own pet dogs. So, you train your dog to recognise a scent which they then search for, detect, and indicate they have found it.

Not only is scentwork great fun for your dog, but it also offers an outlet for their natural desire to sniff and search for scents! It's open to dogs of any age or ability and is possibly one of the most inclusive dog sports because of this.

You can try and start off some basic scentwork at home with your dog. Here's how to play:

Step 1 – Take a small fleecy/soft dog toy that your dog has not yet played with. (fleecy/soft toys are best for this activity because they tend to absorb more scent)

Step 2 – Place the toy into a clean, airtight box, and cover it in dried catnip. (yes, the stuff that cats go crazy for!)

Step 3 – Place the lid on the box tightly, to try and keep the scent of the catnip inside it as much as possible. (clippable lunch boxes can work well for this)

Step 4 – Leave the toy inside the catnip box for 24-48 hours so that the scent of it can become imprinted onto the toy.

Step 5 – Introduce the toy to your dog and encourage them to pick it up and play with it.

Step 6 – Place the toy on the other side of the room in full view and ask your dog to 'find it.'

Step 7 – Increase the difficulty, but only once you are certain your dog has got the hang of finding the toy. You can eventually hide the toy underneath blankets, under your garden bench, behind a radiator, behind a plant pot, etc.

Step 8 – Always place your toy back into the catnip box when you are finished so the scent can sink into it again. If you need to wash the toy at some point, no problem, just leave it in the tub for 1-2 days again afterwards to 'reset.'

High Scent Profile Items – Ideal for: Sniffing & mental stimulation

Items with a high scent profile are basically things with unusual or interesting smells to them that your dog may not come across on a day-to-day basis. Examples could include;

- Horse items - brushes, lead ropes, feed buckets, etc.
- Baby items - rattles, bibs, soft toys, clothing, etc.
- Small animal bedding - hay from a rabbit hutch, fluffy bedding from a hamster, etc.
- Used dog toys – anything that's been played with by other dogs
- Feathers/Fur – from different animals
- Novel items - such as whole coconuts, ice cubes, a skateboard, a stepping stool, and robotic toys that move and make sounds can all add interesting scents for your dog to explore.

Try to be creative here, anything that you think might be interesting for your dog to sniff and interact with. The aim is to give their nose something new and novel to smell which gives their brain something new to process. Introducing exciting new smells like this is an excellent thing to do for your dog!

Muffin Tray Game – Ideal for: Sniffing & mental stimulation

Muffin trays can be a great enrichment tool as they can be filled with different textures and treats in each section. For example, scrunched newspaper in one, hay in another, fabric pieces in the third, and so on all with treats hidden amongst them. You can even cover the treats with tennis balls too, so your dog has to pick them up or paw them out of the way to access the treats. Smaller dogs may find it easier to use an egg box instead.

Treats In A Towel – Ideal for: Sniffing & mental stimulation

This is a really straightforward game to rustle up in minutes at home. All you need is an old towel or blanket and some treats. Here's what you need to do:

Step 1 - Simply fold the towel into 4 with each layer containing treats to start with and encourage your dog to sniff them out.

Step 2 - Once they have got the hang of this, you can fold the towel up into more sections to increase the difficulty.

Step 3 – You can knot the towel loosely to make it more difficult, or put the folded towel into a cardboard box to make it trickier for your dog to access the treats.

Step 4 – If you are feeling creative, try cutting the old towel or blanket into strips. Gather the strips together and tie a knot at one end. Then, plait the fabric until you reach the end and tie a knot in that end to keep it all together. You should now have a plaited toy, which you can use to push treats into, then encourage your dog to sniff out and eat them.

NOTE: It doesn't matter if your dog paws at the towel, or tries to grab it with their teeth, whatever they want to do to access the treats is great!

Hanging Toilet Roll Tubes – Ideal for: Sniffing & mental stimulation

This is a similar concept to the hanging cups game we looked at earlier, but this time using empty toilet roll tubes. This can make it easier for your dog to shred the cardboard tubes if they would like to, to access the treats, which adds another element of interest to the game.

Thread treat-filled toilet roll tubes onto some string and tie them up at your dog's head level. Then encourage them to push the tubes around to release the treats. This reduces their ability to use their feet to pin down the tube, making them rely on just using their mouth, which is more interesting for them, and it will take them longer to access the treats. Remember, if your dog is finding it frustrating, you can help them or make the game easier for them so they can succeed.

Puzzle Toys – Ideal for: Sniffing & mental stimulation

There are several leading brands of puzzle toys, but they are becoming increasingly more widely available. Most commonly they involve hiding small pieces of food within the puzzle and your dog then has to figure out how to access them. It is important to start off at an easy level to introduce your dog to puzzle toys so that you are setting them up to succeed. If the puzzle is too difficult, it is likely to increase their frustration levels and cause them to lose interest which is something we want to avoid.

Dog-Safe Herbs – Ideal for: Sniffing & mental stimulation

A good place to start could be setting aside a small section of your garden to grow some dog-safe herbs. These can be planted directly in the ground or grown in pots. Some people grow different herbs in small pots hung on their fences or walls at their dog's height. It's best to keep the herbs separate from each other if possible so your dog can choose which one they want to sniff. If they don't like the smell of lavender but love mint, and they are grown together, it can make them not want to sniff the mint either. Make sure any herbs you choose are safe for your dog to not only sniff, but also eat in case they decide to chew on them! Good examples include: Basil, Mint (***Pennyroyal mint - Mentha Pulegium - is toxic to dogs, so avoid this!),*** Dandelions, Lemon Balm, Lavender, Chamomile, Thyme, Parsley, and Wheatgrass.

Some dogs actively seek out herbs and plants to self-soothe if they are feeling under the weather. Although many people already know that dogs tend to eat grass if they are feeling sick, there is actually a lot more to this than you may realise. The art of self-medication in animals is known as Zoopharmacognosy and this is when your dog will choose what they need to help themselves feel better. So, if they are feeling anxious, they may choose to sniff lavender. Or, if they are having digestive issues, they may eat some Wheatgrass. This is a very basic and generalised overview of Zoopharmacognosy but it does help explain the benefits of having dog-safe herbs and plants available for your dog to interact with. If you would like to learn more about Zoopharmacognosy then I would recommend Caroline Ingraham's book 'Help Your Dog Heal Itself.' Caroline is the founder of Applied Zoopharmacognosy and she has extensively researched and studied the effects and benefits of bringing natural remedies to animals who are not free to forage them for themselves.

Unfortunately, not everything your dog sniffs and eats will be in their best interests, so it's still important that they only have access to plants and herbs that are safe for them.

Enrichment Ideas For Dogs Who Love To Shred

Shredding items is actually a very natural behaviour for our dogs. It forms part of the canine predatory sequence but in this it is referred to as dissection. So, when a dog is hunting, they orient themselves, eye & stalk the prey, chase, grab-bite, kill-bite, dissect, and then consume. This dissection part of the process involves the dog ripping the hair/fur/feathers/flesh from the animal so they can consume it, and it is this part of the process that makes them love shredding things so much! Here are some ideas for enrichment activities for dogs who love to shred:

Cuddly Toys – Ideal for: Playing & shredding

These are a real favourite of my dogs and so I often purchase teddies from charity shops for them to play with. Care should be taken to remove any hard plastic eyes or noses from the teddies, as they can be a danger to your dog if they swallow them. It is also advisable to avoid those with 'beans' in them as a stuffing material, as again they can easily be ingested accidentally. So many people say 'I won't give my dogs cuddly toys because all they do is rip them up' but I would argue that that is actually all part of the fun! Just be prepared to pick up bits of stuffing afterwards and as with any toy, you should supervise your dog whilst they are playing with them and remove them when they are damaged.

Pass The Parcel – Ideal for: Shredding

Treats can be wrapped in newspaper to form a 'present' similar to the 'pass the parcel' game where each layer of the parcel contains small amounts of treats and/or toys. Your dog then has to shred the parcel open to access the treats. Start by putting plenty of treats and wrapping the present loosely without any tape so it's easier for your dog to rip up and access the treats. You can then add more layers and/or fewer treats and wrap the present tighter to increase the difficulty once your dog has got the hang of what to do.

Wrapping Presents – Ideal for: Playing & shredding

Many dogs enjoy ripping open presents – I mean, who doesn't love presents? If they have been treated to a new toy, consider wrapping it up before you give it to them and encourage them to open it. You can even wrap up one of their current toys in some old newspaper and let them shred the paper off to get to their favourite toy!

Treats In A Paper Bag – Ideal for: Sniffing & shredding

Wrap some tasty treats up in a paper bag and encourage your dog to shred it to access the treats. You can stuff the bag with some newspaper to increase the difficulty level. If you are concerned about them eating parts of the paper bag, you could try wrapping the treats in a large cabbage or lettuce leaf instead.

Toilet Roll Tubes – Ideal for: Sniffing & shredding

Collect your cardboard toilet rolls, kitchen rolls, or wrapping paper tubes and stuff them with newspaper or shredded paper, and hide treats inside. If you have several, you could even arrange them inside a cardboard box to increase the difficulty level. It's not a problem if your dog shreds the toilet roll tubes in the process, this is all part of the fun.

Lucky Dip (Shoe Box With Shredded Paper) – Ideal for: Sniffing & shredding

Most of us always seem to have a cardboard box lying around the house and this can be a great form of enrichment. Simply fill them with old newspaper or magazines then scatter in some dry treats or kibble to encourage your dog to sniff them out. It doesn't matter if they rip the box, that is all part of the fun! Just be prepared to tidy up afterwards. Start by leaving a few treats in view on the top layer of the box, to give your dog the idea that there might be more where they came from if they investigate a little deeper into the box!

Enrichment Ideas For Dogs Who Love To Lick & Chew

The process of licking and chewing is extremely relaxing for your dog and can help them unwind and settle down. This is why some dogs lick themselves when they are feeling a little bit stressed, to help themselves feel better. Anxious dogs can be especially licky, sometimes to the point of obsession where they constantly lick themselves, you, other dogs, the floor, furniture etc in a desperate bid to soothe themselves and feel calmer. If we can provide our dogs with plenty of enrichment activities which involve licking and chewing, it can really help them to relax. Here are some suggestions to try:

Lick Mats – Ideal for: Sniffing & licking

Lick mats are usually silicone-type mats which contain different raised designs on them. These are then smothered in wet food, raw food, meat pastes etc. and your dog is encouraged to lick the contents from the mat. The different textures are interesting for your dog and because they are getting a food reward, it is reinforcing for them to repeat the process. Lick mats can also double as useful training aids, as they can be placed at the side of a bath when your dog is being washed, or on the wall when they are being groomed for example, to create a positive experience for them while keeping them entertained.

Ice Cube Tray – Ideal for: Sniffing & licking

These are ideal for smaller dogs or for a quick version of a lick mat which you may already have at home! They can be used in the same way as lick mats by spreading food over them and encouraging your dog to lick them. You can get different-shaped ice cube or ice lolly moulds, all of which are cheap alternatives to lick mats.

Stuffed Kongs – Ideal for: Sniffing & licking

Kong is a brand that makes rubber toys which can be filled with wet food, meat pastes, cream cheese, dog-safe peanut butter, or other spreadable treats which your dog has to lick and chew on in order to access their treats. Once your dog has got the hang of it, these filled food toys could even be frozen so that it increases the difficulty level by it taking your dog longer to access the food.

Even though Kongs and similar products are considered quite durable toys, they are not indestructible. So, it's best not to leave your dog unattended with them, especially if they are a powerful chewer.

NOTE: Many human peanut butter products contain Xylitol which is an artificial sweetener often found in confectionery products. Xylitol is toxic to our dogs, which is why it's so essential they do not ingest it. A dog's body confuses this sugar substitute for actual sugar, resulting in more insulin being released than is needed, causing their blood sugar levels to plummet to dangerously low levels. This is known as Hypoglycaemia, and it can be fatal. Xylitol is often found in chewing gums, mouthwashes, human toothpastes, sugar free desserts, low-calorie baked goods (as these often contain sweeteners instead of real sugar) and certain spreads like nut butters. You can purchase peanut butter made especially for dogs which shouldn't contain anything potentially harmful for your dog. So, be sure to always read the ingredients and avoid anything which contains Xylitol or Birch Sugar as it is also sometimes known.

Lick The Pot – Ideal for: Sniffing & licking

Most dogs would love the chance to lick an empty yoghurt pot clean! Make sure the product you give them to lick is dog-safe of course! So, next time you get to the end of your cream cheese, yoghurt, pate, etc. consider letting your dog make sure the pot is clean enough to recycle! My dogs queue up when they know there might be a yoghurt pot heading in their direction!

Natural Chews – Ideal for: Licking & chewing

An enrichment activity that is often overlooked is giving your dog something delicious to chew on! Choose a natural, long-lasting treat that is suitable for your dog's age and size. Good examples are dried chicken feet, beef pizzles, dried fish skins, rabbit ears, and yak snacks (hard, dried cheese bars).

My dogs love a bedtime snack of a chicken foot before bed, it gives them something tasty to crunch on and it settles them down beautifully for their night's sleep. So much so, when they hear the jar of chicken feet open, they run upstairs into the bedroom ready for bedtime snacks!

Remember to avoid any products containing rawhide! They are exceptionally difficult for your dog to digest properly and often contain unhealthy chemicals, flavourings, and preservatives. They can even cause intestinal blockages because they are not easily digested, especially if your dog swallows large chunks of them at once.

It's also generally advised to avoid giving your dog any natural chews that you cannot dent with your fingernail. So, I would be cautious about giving them hooves, antlers, filled calcium bones, and other exceptionally hard chews. Although they will certainly last longer, they have been known to damage dog's teeth or their jaw as they chew on them.

Durable Toys – Ideal for: Licking, chewing & playing

Durable, hard-wearing toys are great for your dog to chew on. Choose materials like rope or rubber for longer-lasting toys. These are also great for teething puppies, as they can be frozen before being given to your pup, to help soothe their sore gums. Make sure you don't leave your dog with toys unattended just in case they do manage to chew any bits off them!

Even toys that are marketed as being indestructible are likely not! Especially if your dog is a real power chewer. To try and reduce the chance of your dog destroying the toy in minutes, make sure their other needs are being met beforehand. Make sure they have had enough physical exercise, and have had time to wind down before you give them their chew toy. This should help reduce any pent-up energy and frustration which can contribute to your dog chewing strongly with the intention of destroying the toy.

Enrichment Ideas For Dogs Who Love Food

Most dogs LOVE food, that's hard to deny! So, why not use this to your advantage and provide your dog with something interesting to do? As tempting as it is to give your dog lots of treats just for being the cutest dog around (which is all dogs, all the time!) sometimes it's better for them to participate in an exciting activity to get their paws on these treats. Even dogs who are not always hugely motivated by food or treats, may well show much more interest if their food is presented in novel or unusual ways. This is because it taps into their natural instincts more so than simply having all their meals given to them each day! So, here are some ideas of different enrichment activities to try if your dog loves food:

Novel Tasting Platters – Ideal for: Sniffing & eating

A great form of enrichment is allowing your dog to taste different foods that they may not have access to on a day-to-day basis. Suggestions of items to fill your platter with could be; fruits, vegetables (cooked and raw), meat paste, cooked or raw meats or fish, dehydrated treats, and cheese spread. Anything goes really! As many different tastes and textures as possible are the aims here, though ***take care to avoid anything that may be unsuitable for your dog to consume.***

NOTE: Unsuitable foods for your dog includes: onions, leeks, garlic (although garlic in dog-specific supplements is okay to give to your dog, I wouldn't recommend giving them fresh or cooked garlic), chocolate (as this contains theobromine which can cause kidney failure. The darker the chocolate, the higher the risk), macadamia nuts, avocado, raisins, currants, sultanas, grapes, cooked bones (because they can easily splinter when your dog chews them).

You can create your platter in your dog's bowl, on a flat dinner plate, on an old chopping board, or even directly on the ground, whatever works best for you! You only have to provide a small amount of each food item and if possible, leave space in between each item so your dog can actively choose what they would like to eat. You will see that most dogs (no matter how greedy they usually are!) will take time to sniff each item briefly before deciding which order to eat them in. You will soon learn what your dog likes and doesn't like, though just because they have refused something this time doesn't mean they will never like it, they might just not fancy trying it at the time! Our dog's tastes change over time, just like ours do, so it's important to provide them with interesting tastes regularly to make their diet more interesting.

As humans, we are creatures of habit and we tend to find ourselves sticking to the same flavoured kibble our dog has eaten for years, day in, day out because they 'like it' and it's easier for us. However, even if they do like it, it doesn't mean they would like a change every now and again, if their dietary requirements allow for it.

For example, the vast majority of dog food manufacturers have a choice of different proteins available for you to choose from. So, provided your dog doesn't have any sensitivities, intolerances, or allergies to certain foods, it's a good idea to mix them up a bit. So, choose your dog's favourite kibble made with fish, then swap to turkey, then to duck and so on. This adds some variation to your dog's diet and stops it from becoming monotonous for them. As much as you might enjoy a certain kind of cereal, I am sure you would soon be craving something different if you ate that for every meal, every day, for weeks on end!

Food Toys – Ideal for: Sniffing, eating & mental stimulation

The most common form of food toy would be a ball in which you place kibble pieces or dry treats; your dog should then be encouraged to move the ball around, in turn releasing the food. This then acts as a reward and incentive for them to continue to play with the ball. There are several different kinds of food toys available on the market including some which wobble when your dog hits them, and then return to upright, some that spin, some that roll forwards and backwards, and many more. So, experiment to find out which your dog likes interacting with best!

Scatter Feeding – Ideal for: Sniffing, foraging & eating

A simple enrichment idea is to scatter your dog's food or treats in the garden, yard, house, or out on walks so they have to sniff out their snacks. As with any enrichment activity, it is important to set your dog up for success, particularly when they are trying something new. The difficulty level can then be increased gradually once they have gained confidence in the task.

Scatter feeding can also be beneficial if your dog is reactive too. If you are out on a walk and come across a trigger (another dog, horse, person, car, or whatever it may be) then sprinkle a few snacks on the ground around your dog to give them something to focus on. Provided the trigger is far enough way to keep your dog under their tolerance threshold, they should happily sniff out the treats and eat them, which will help to keep them calm.

Plastic Bottles – Ideal for: Sniffing, eating & mental stimulation

Every house has an empty plastic bottle at some point, so you can use this as a make-your-own interactive food toy. Simply cut small holes all over the bottle, and fill it with dried treats or kibble. Encourage your dog to move the bottle around so that the treats fall out to reward them. To begin with, make sure there are plenty of large holes so the treats fall out relatively easily, then the holes can be reduced in size and number as they get the hang of it, to increase the difficulty level. One of my dogs is particularly crafty and has worked out that she can quickly chew the top off the bottle and tip all the treats out in one go – genius!

Treat Bobbing – Sniffing, eating & mental stimulation

Like the human version of 'apple-bobbing' you can drop treats into a bowl or bucket of shallow water and encourage your dog to fish them out. They can use their mouth or their paws, whichever they prefer! Be careful because they may tip the water everywhere, so this is an outside activity! Try to use some treats that float and some that sink for variety and variation.

Slow Feeder Bowls – Sniffing, eating & mental stimulation

There is more to slow feeder bowls than simply slowing down how fast your dog eats their food! They can be spread with different soft foods, in the same way as a lick mat, which encourages your dog to carefully lick the food from them. The different textures, surfaces, and materials used in slow feeder bowls make them much more interactive for your dog compared with a standard bowl. They can also help to aid digestion which is great news for dogs who usually gobble their food down in one mouthful and give themselves wind, or make themselves feel sick in the process! Slowing your dog down when they're eating not only helps them to digest their food more effectively, but it can also keep them calmer as they are not frantically trying to inhale their food in 5 seconds!

Enrichment Ideas For Dogs Who Love To Learn

Some dogs, particularly the working breeds generally, love to learn new things! Their active brains need to be challenged and teaching them something new can be just what they need. The possibilities of what you can teach your dog to do are truly limitless. Anything you can think of, you can probably teach your dog to do it if you use the right methods and have the patience to work through the steps involved. So, if you are teaching a basic behaviour, or something much more complex, keep things positive and take it one step at a time. Reward your dog for small successes and build from there, and before you know it, you will have achieved your goal! Here are some enrichment activities for dogs who love to learn:

Trick Training – Ideal for: Mental stimulation & bond-building

Trick training not only gives your dog's brain a good workout; but it is also likely to improve the relationship you share with them. Plus, who can say no to a dog who wants you to shake their paw in return for a biscuit? As with all training, when teaching your dog tricks, this should be done using positive reinforcement methods, in order to maintain your dog's happiness and increase their chance of learning them successfully. Science proves that if you reward your dog for showing desirable behaviours, they are more likely to show this behaviour again in the future!

While this is not a book specifically about training, here are a few tricks to consider teaching your dog:

- **Touch** – Hold your hand out with a flat palm and teach your dog to nudge their nose into it as a 'touch.' This can be useful to get your dog's attention and encourage them to check in with you.
- **Spin/Twist** – Choose one cue for your dog to turn 360 degrees clockwise and the other for anticlockwise. This helps to encourage your dog to be aware of their entire body, and not just prioritise their front legs.
- **Both Paws** – Choose a different cue for each paw, perhaps paw for one and shake for the other. Encourage your dog to lift their paw into your hand to 'shake it.' This encourages your dog to use both paws because dogs naturally tend to use one side more than the other as a default, just as we do as humans.
- **Beg** – Get your dog to sit and encourage them to sit up and 'beg' by luring them with a treat. Reward any small successes to start off with as this is a difficult trick to learn if they have never done it before. It's great for promoting your dog's balance and core strength.

Freestyling – Ideal for: Mental stimulation & bond-building

This is something that I LOVE to do with my own dogs! It gives them the opportunity to think for themselves and try new things to see if you will reward them for doing so. My youngest dog Delta, has learned a large portion of her known tricks through freestyling. For this, your dog needs to have a good understanding of what clicker training and positive reinforcement is to get the best results. Here is what you need to do:

Step 1 – Get your dog to do a few basic behaviours that they already know and can do easily i.e. sit, paw, down, etc. and reward them for it. This gets them into the headspace for learning and thinking and sets the tone for what is about to come next.

Step 2 – Next, ask your dog 'what can you do?' and see if they offer any behaviours up for you.

Step 3 – You may find that they offer easy behaviours for them, so even if they are very basic tricks, still reward them as they are thinking for themselves about what they can do, and this is exactly what we want them to do!

Step 4 – If your dog continually offers the same behaviour repeatedly, only reward them for it once, to encourage them to try something different next time.

Step 5 – Once your dog understands that they need to think for themselves, you may be surprised at the behaviours they start offering to you. As soon as they show something you want to see more of, mark and reward this behaviour and give it a cue.

Heelwork To Music – Ideal for: Mental stimulation & bond-building

Also affectionately known as 'doggy dancing' this is the sort of thing that you see dogs doing on TV talent shows! Now, not every dog will be able to compete in talent competitions, but there is no harm in teaching your dog some of the more basic moves at home. This will keep their brain busy, give them some mental enrichment and encourage them to move their body in different ways too. Here are some examples that you could teach your dog to do:

- **Spin & Twist** - These are basic moves and are a good place to start.
- **Middle** – This is where your dog stands in between your legs, looking up at you. You can then progress this to your dog walking in this position, as you are walking forward and backwards.
- **Touch My Feet** – This is when your dog touches your feet with their paw when you hold your foot forward. Have them facing you and encourage them to touch their opposite paw onto the foot you have put forward for them.
- **Weave Through Legs** – Stand with your legs wide apart and lure your dog in a figure of 8 motion through your leg, round the side, back through your legs and so on.
- **Conga** – A bit like the conga dance move, encourage your dog to jump up and rest their front feet onto your back (if they are tall

enough!) and then keep them there while you move forwards.

Tidy Up Your Toys – Ideal for: Mental stimulation & bond-building

It's likely your dog already has lots of toys dotted around the house! If it's anything like my house, the doggy toy box is usually empty and instead the toys are all over the place! But, at the end of the day, you can encourage your dog to tidy up their toys and put them back into their toybox. Here's how to teach your dog how to tidy up:

Step 1 – Get your dog's toybox and several toys ready. Keep the toys on the floor close to the toybox to start off with to make it easier for your dog to succeed.
Step 2 – Encourage your dog to pick up a toy and when they are near the toybox, ask them to 'leave' the toy. This should mean that the toy is dropped into the toybox.
Step 3 – Repeat this again with the other toys until they are all put away.
Step 4 – Once your dog understands the idea of what you are trying to do, you can repeat the process with toys that are further away from the toybox.

NOTE: You could also mimic this training for other areas of your dog's life and create a mutually beneficial arrangement for you and your dog in the process. For example, teach your dog to pick up an empty plastic bottle and take it to your recycling bin.

Or teach them to pick up your worn clothes and put them into the washing basket.

Learn Toys By Name – Ideal for: Mental stimulation & bond-building

Some dogs love to learn their toys by name and this can be a wonderful way to get them thinking. Here is how you can teach your dog to know their toys by name:

Step 1 – Choose your dog's favourite toy. For this analogy, we will use a tennis ball.
Step 2 – Put the ball on the floor and encourage your dog to pick up the ball and say 'Ball' as they grab it.
Step 3 – Play a fun game with the ball as a reward for them picking it up.
Step 4 – Choose your dog's second favourite toy. We will use a teddy for this.
Step 5 – Put the teddy on the floor and encourage your dog to pick up the teddy and say 'Teddy' as they grab it.
Step 6 – Play a fun game with the teddy as a reward for them picking it up.
Step 7 – Repeat this process with more of your dog's toys, making sure they all have distinct names which are easy for your dog to distinguish between.
Step 8 – Once your dog understands the names of several toys, you can make it more difficult for them by asking them to fetch the 'ball' from a selection of toys on the ground.

Hoopers – Ideal for: Mental stimulation, bond-building & physical exercise

Hoopers is one of the newer dog sports available for you to participate in. It is similar to agility but is a much lower-impact version because there are no jumps or contact equipment for your dog to navigate. Instead, the aim is to get your dog through a series of hoops, barrels, and tunnels; hence the name hoopers. It is one of the UK's fastest-growing dog sports because it is fun and gives your dog's brain and body a workout without the tight turns and higher risk of injury that can come with agility. Because it is so low impact (no jumping/risk of falling off contact equipment etc), hoopers is much more accessible to dogs of different ages, sizes, and abilities than other more traditional dog sports. Pups from as young as 6 months can take part in hoopers, and it's great for older dogs to work through at their own pace too. Many dogs who have now retired from competitive agility or flyball turn to hoopers as a way of still keeping them enriched at a more manageable and safer level.

Enrichment Ideas For Dogs Who Love To Run & Jump

There are very few dogs who don't love to run freely. It's one of the most heart-warming things you can see in life when you see your dog joyfully running as fast as they can towards you. It's like something from a fairy-tale, apart from this is reality! Remember, we are free to move around the world in any way that we want, if we fancy going for a run, we can without restraint. Though sadly, this is often not the case for many dogs, who spend their lives either confined to their home, or attached to a lead and unable to move freely.

Although it is not safe or responsible to let your dog run freely if they don't have a reliable recall, there are some options to consider below while you are working on improving your dog's recall.

Doggy Parkour – Ideal for: Physical exercise, mental stimulation & jumping

Although canine parkour is not as extreme as the human version, where people free run across the tops of buildings, it is still a fantastic way to encourage your dog to explore the environment around them. The beauty of this is, you can adapt it completely to suit whatever is happening around you. So, no matter if you are walking down a busy high street, in a quiet woodland, in a field, or even in your own backyard, you can use elements of parkour anywhere.

NOTE: It's important to consider your dog's size, general fitness, and health status before doing doggy parkour. Giant breeds may find it easy to jump up onto things but can struggle to get down again without putting strain on their joints in the process. Small or toy breeds may find it difficult to jump onto high things and can risk injuring themselves if they were to fall from a height. Dogs with known weaknesses or proneness to issues should be monitored closely too. For example, Dachshunds who can easily damage their long backs, shouldn't be encouraged to jump up onto anything high. So, it's essential you tailor doggy parkour to your dog's own needs to minimise any risks.

The aim is to encourage your dog to explore as many different heights, textures, and viewpoints as possible. This makes their walks much more interesting and interactive for them. So, look out for benches that your dog can jump on, tree stumps for them to sit on, bollards for them to weave around, tree trunks for them to jump up and lean on, bike racks for them to walk through, and anything else that you can creatively think of to enrich your dog's walk with. The encouragement and teamwork that's involved with parkour also help to reinforce the relationship you share with your dog, as the fun activities are coming from you working together.

Agility – Ideal for: Physical exercise, mental stimulation, bond-building & jumping

Agility is a great way to get your dog's body moving and keep their mind active. Agility consists of jumps, tunnels, long jumps, A-frames, dog-walks, and weaves that your dog needs to navigate as part of a course. It can help improve your dog's fitness levels, gives them mental stimulation, and encourages you to work together as a team. The basics can be done at home, or you could go to classes if you want to take things further or even enter competitions in the future. For agility, you need to make sure that your dog is fully developed skeletally so it shouldn't be done with young puppies who are still growing as you risk damaging their joints with the impact involved. Remember, agility should always be fun for your dog and they should never be forced to do it.

Flyball – Ideal for: Physical exercise, mental stimulation, bond-building & jumping

Flyball consists of a series of 4 jumps set out in a line, your dog has to jump these and then retrieve a tennis ball from a 'flyball box.' This tennis ball must then be carried back over the same 4 jumps and the dog then returns back to you. Flyball is a team sport, with each team consisting of 4 dogs. The aim is to get each of the 4 dogs to complete their leg of the run, one after another, in the fastest time possible. There are also two lanes next to each other, where a second team of dogs are also competing at the same time as you. Flyball is a high-intensity, fast-paced sport with little room for error and a lot of dogs absolutely love it! It doesn't matter if your dog is small, big, fast, or slow, they are all still valuable assets to a flyball team.

Free Running – Ideal for: Physical exercise, mental stimulation & running

Having the opportunity to run freely is something every dog should be allowed to do as often as possible. Even if your dog doesn't have a reliable recall yet, or if they don't like being around other dogs, there are loads of secure dog-walking fields popping up across the country. This gives your dog a safe space where they can run freely and really explore their environment at their own pace. It gives your dog a chance for a full body workout and for them to move around exactly how they want to, which is not always possible when they are only ever walked on a lead. The fact of reality is, our dogs often walk a lot faster than we can, and cover the ground a lot quicker than we do too. There is nothing quite like seeing your dog running freely!

NOTE: If you feel like you need some help with your dog's recall, you can see a preview of the book 'Rocket Recall' at the end of this book. Rocket Recall is written by my friend and colleague Simone Mueller and is an excellent resource for teaching your dog a reliable rocket recall of their own.

Cani-Cross – Ideal for: Physical exercise, bond-building & running

Cani-Cross is essentially cross-country running with your dog, which makes this a great choice if you are looking to keep fit yourself too! It's thought to have originated from sled dogs who needed to be exercised and kept in peak physical condition in the seasons when they were not actively working. Then, dog owners of other breeds recognised the benefits for their pet dogs too. There are now competitions across the country where dogs and their owners compete for the fastest course times in different categories.

It differs slightly from simply going for a run with your dog because Cani-Cross dogs are fitted with specialist harnesses, which are fastened to their owner by a bungee lead. This is then fastened around the owner's waist via a running belt. The dogs are encouraged to pull into the harness and pull their human partner along in the process.

Cani-Cross is open to any dog breeds to participate, provided they are healthy and able to run, and they have a human who can keep up with them! Start off with short distance runs and build up the duration gradually as both your dog's and your stamina improve.

Bikejor – Ideal for: Physical exercise, bond-building & running

Bikejor is the same basic principle as Cani-Cross, but instead of the human running with their dog, they are riding a bicycle. The dog is then attached via a bungee lead to a specialist pole on the bike. This reduces the risk of the dog running into the bike's wheels and injuring themselves.

Bikejor relies heavily on your dog listening and responding to your directional cues, as well as speed-up and slow-down cues, all of which can be taught to your dog before you get going with this sport.

This activity is growing in popularity throughout the UK now, and there are clubs popping up across the country. So, if you are interested in Bikejor it's best to locate and contact your local club.

Enrichment Ideas For Dogs Who Love To Play

Playing releases feel-good hormones like Dopamine, Oxytocin & Serotonin which make your dog feel happier! So, it's not hard to see why some dogs love to play so much. Dogs are only one of a handful of mammals who continue to play even into their adulthood, so don't think that your older dog won't want to play anymore, this is not something they grow out of.

Playtime encourages your dog to get their body moving, which can help to keep them healthier than those who lead very sedentary lives. It also gives their brain a workout too, which is always a winning combination! It also teaches them about communication, which can help to increase their social awareness.

Here are some enrichment ideas for dogs who love playtime:

Tug Toys – Ideal for: physical exercise, playtime & bond-building

These are not only a good enrichment tool, but they can also strengthen your relationship with your dog through play. Chasing, grabbing, and playing tug-of-war with a toy is highly enriching as it mimics parts of the natural predatory sequence which is rewarding and exciting for your dog. However, because of this, it can leave your dog feeling pretty wound up after a high-intensity game of tug, so you would benefit from following these sessions up with a calmer activity.

Unstructured Play – Ideal for: physical exercise, playtime & bond-building

Play is a vital part of your dog's happiness, and although there are thousands of products available, all with a specific aim in mind, sometimes it is nice for your dog to just simply play for playing sake. Whether that be with other dogs, with you as their owner, or even on their own. Many dogs enjoy playing simply because it makes them feel good, and they enjoy it. So, playtime does not always have to be structured for it to be enriching.

Interactive Toys – Ideal for: physical exercise, playtime & bond-building

There are many toys which emit different sounds such as squeaks or honks, or they crinkle when they are chewed. Some are even battery-operated, and they play music or interesting noises when they are moved around. If your dog likes to play ball, consider getting a differently shaped one so that when it bounces, it goes in different directions, to keep things interesting. Toys that are made up of different textures are also good for enrichment, as the various parts feel different when your dog holds or chews them which adds more interest.

Social Butterflies – Ideal for: physical exercise, playtime, bond-building & socialisation

If your dog is a social butterfly, then it's important that they have the opportunity to spend time with other social dogs. However, it's crucial to remember that this doesn't mean letting them interact with every dog they meet or allowing them to charge up to unknown dogs to play, no matter how friendly your dog may be. This is considered very rude behaviour and not every dog wants to play with, or interact with other dogs, and that is perfectly fine! There is often a huge amount of pressure on owners to make sure their dog is friendly with other dogs and happy to be fussed by strangers, however the reality is that some dogs simply don't feel comfortable doing this. In the same way as some humans are naturally more reserved and others are more outgoing, this is the same as for our dogs.

However, if your dog does love to play with other dogs, it's a good idea to arrange to meet up with other dogs of a similar nature, who would both benefit from some playtime with each other. Even if these dogs know each other well, it's essential you keep an eye on the body language of both of them, to make absolutely sure they are both comfortable for play to continue.

Toy Rotation – Ideal for: playtime & mental stimulation

Many of us have loads of toys for our dogs, and they can't possibly play with them all at once! Consider rotating your dog's toy collection, so some are kept to one side, and then reintroduced in replacement of their current options. This keeps their interest levels high. You could also let your dog choose their own toys, for example, give them a selection of 5 different toys to play with and have a fun game with whichever one they decide on.

Your Involvement – Ideal for: playtime, mental stimulation & bond-building

Although this is not strictly a recommendation for a specific toy or game, it's often the case that your dog will be much more interested in playing, if you are involved in the game too! While some dogs will happily entertain themselves with a toy on their own, some would much prefer you to be playing the game with them. For example, if you leave a toy on the floor, your dog may not show any interest. But, if you grabbed the toy and started dragging it across the floor, it's likely your dog would become more animated and want to get involved in what you are doing. The toy itself hasn't changed; they are just interested in it now because you are showing an active interest too.

Enrichment Ideas For Dogs Who Love To Relax

Relaxation is something that is often overlooked, especially when you are thinking about enrichment. There is often a larger emphasis on keeping your dog busy, giving them something to do and exercising their body and mind. And while of course, this is important, it's essential your dog has time to relax and rest too.

Pushing your dog's physical exercise and mental stimulation levels further and further won't create a happy and contented canine if they never have the chance to fully unwind and calm down. Relaxation and sleep are essential to your dog's overall happiness and well-being. Not only this, it is crucial for them to be able to process any new learning or information effectively. If your dog is constantly on the go, looking for the next activity, this is not a sustainable way for them to live.

Some dogs need to be actively encouraged and taught how to relax and unwind, and the ideas we will look at below should hopefully help you to teach them how to do this.

Playing Music – Ideal for: relaxation

There is some research into the benefits of musical enrichment for dogs. It's thought that classical music is calming for dogs and helps them relax, although some dogs may prefer different genres. Studies are quite limited on this idea, but the ones that have been carried out suggest that there are likely calming benefits, and it's unlikely to have any negative effects. So, this would make it a cheap and straightforward way to positively impact your dog's life.

Leaving music playing for your dog when you leave them can also help to lessen any background noises which can disturb your dog, meaning they can enjoy a more restful snooze without interruptions. There are even playlists on music streaming services that are specially designed for dogs! So, you would need to experiment to see what your dog's preferences are.

Watching The Environment – Ideal for: relaxation & bond-building

Sometimes it's nice to just sit and watch the world go by, without anything specific to do or anywhere important to be. Time to just catch your breath and have a moment of calm. And your dog would benefit from this too! So, next time you are out for a walk, take a moment to find somewhere to sit or stand and let your dog take in what is happening around them. Sharing this momentary calmness between you and your dog is beneficial for both of you and can help strengthen the bond you share with each other.

You could also add some 'Islands of Relaxation' to your dog's walk. This means that when you reach your chosen 'island' or point on your walk, your dog is free to enjoy some calming enrichment activities in this area. This should be something that occurs every time your dog reaches these destinations, so they know what to expect. For example, you could choose a quiet spot in a woodland, a calm corner of a field, a sheltered picnic bench, etc and scatter some treats on the ground for your dog to snuffle out. This can reduce your dog's stress levels and keep them feeling calmer for the rest of your walk.

Massage – Ideal for: relaxation & bond-building

Learning some basic massage techniques can be really soothing and relaxing for your dog. Simple things like rubbing their ears, or giving them long, slow, strokes across the length of their body can be good places to start. Every dog will have different preferences of where they like being touched, so what one dog may love, another dog may not like at all. So, have a think about what your dog enjoys when you are fussing them and see if you can replicate this as calming massage technique.

Comfy Resting Places – Ideal for: relaxation

Now, this is not necessarily an enrichment activity as such, but it is still a particularly important point to mention. It is vital that your dog has access to comfortable resting places that they can go to whenever they feel like they need some time out or some sleep. There is often a huge emphasis put on keeping your dog busy, giving them things to do and interacting with them constantly, but sometimes, all your dog really wants to do is go for a quiet nap, somewhere comfortable where they won't be disturbed. Some dogs prefer the safety of a crate with a comfortable bed inside, others prefer to sleep on your sofa, and some may like a bed under the stairs or in a corner of your room. Wherever your dog chooses, make sure they always have free access to it. Consider your dog's age, size, and general preferences when thinking about the type of bed you give to them.

Just like us, without the opportunity to rest and relax effectively, your dog can become irritable, tired, and more likely to overreact to things they can otherwise tolerate.

Quality Time Together – Ideal for: relaxation & bond-building

This is something that is often overlooked in favour of more 'exciting' enrichment activities, but it really is a brilliant and important one. Make time each day to spend some genuine quality time with your dog. You don't need to be doing anything exciting or interesting during this time, just you and your dog, hanging out together and enjoying each other's company. Some dogs sadly lead very lonely lives, often waiting home-alone for their owner to come back from work, only to greet them briefly, before they are back out of the door again for their next engagement. So, if your dog is craving attention, let them have it in abundance from you! After all, our dogs rely on us totally for everything in their life, including the amount of love and affection they receive from their people.

My dogs love nothing more than a cuddle on the sofa with us in the evening. They love the feeling of being close to us, sitting with us, and being in our company and I have to admit, I love this too! There is something very soothing about seeing your dog completely relaxed and at ease in your company and that is exactly how it should be!

Enrichment Ideas For Dogs Who Love To Dig

There are many reasons why dogs love to dig including; to relieve boredom, because it's instinctual behaviour, to reduce stress, to bury a highly-valued treat or toy, to try and escape from the area they are in, to search for prey, or simply because they enjoy it, and it makes them feel good! Whatever the reason is behind your dog's digging, lots of dogs simply love it!

Some dog breeds have even been encouraged to dig through selective breeding, such as Terriers and certain Hounds, who will often dig the ground quickly in search of prey.

So, providing your dog with a safe place to exercise this desire is a great thing to do for them. And, despite what some may think, encouraging your dog to dig in their own specific areas, won't increase the chance of them wanting to dig elsewhere in more undesirable places. In fact, because you are providing an outlet for their natural needs, it's more likely to reduce unwanted digging of your flower beds and flooring!

Here are some enrichment ideas for dogs who love to dig:

Ball Pool – Ideal for: mental stimulation, playtime & digging

A children's plastic paddling pool can make a great enrichment game for your dog, especially when you fill it with plastic play balls. Many dogs will enjoy diving in to retrieve a toy, or snuffling around to find scattered treats amongst the balls. Doing this will also increase their confidence, so if they are reluctant to go in at first, don't be tempted to pick them up and put them in or force them to, they will go in when they are ready. If you don't have plastic play balls, you can fill the pool with empty plastic bottles instead for a cheaper option.

If your dog wants to dig the plastic balls or bottles out of their ball pool, that is absolutely fine! In fact, this is exactly what they will likely want to do! Just be prepared for tidying up afterwards!

A ball pool can also double up as a paddling pool on warmer days, which will not only help your dog to cool down but will also provide them with some much-needed mental stimulation if it is too hot to take them for a walk. You could add extra interest by adding toys that sink, as well as ones that float to encourage your dog to search for them.

Sandpits – Ideal for: mental stimulation, playtime & digging

These can be a permanent fixture in your garden if space allows, or something that you can tidy away again if you need more room. Again, children's plastic paddling pools make great sandpits for dogs who love to dig. Or you can build your own using wooden sleepers, lined with plastic too. Choose kid-friendly sand to fill it as builder's grade sand will often stain your dog's fur orange! Or you could opt for woodchip, so long as you are certain that your dog won't try and eat it. Be prepared for sand flying everywhere though! It's a good idea to get a cover or a lid for your sandpit too, so that it doesn't become water-logged in the rain.

X Marks The Spot – Ideal for: mental stimulation, playtime, bond-building & digging

You can simulate a treasure hunt with your dog where you bury a toy or some treats in something and encourage them to dig it up! This requires them to sniff out the location of the treats, as well as digging to access them properly. You could leave a trail of lower-value treats (i.e. kibble or dried biscuit treats) which lead your dog to the 'treasure' of the higher-value treat (i.e. air-dried meat, cooked meats, etc) which will be lightly buried. This means they can still smell the buried treasure, but can't see it immediately. Making use of mole hills that you come across is a great option for this game when you are out walking!

Help Me Garden – Ideal for: Mental stimulation, bond-building & digging

Teach your dog to dig on cue, so they can 'help' you when you are working in the garden. This benefits both of you, as it gives your dog an outlet for their desire to dig and will get your jobs done faster in the process!

Here's how you can teach your dog to dig on cue:
Step 1 – Find a clear patch of soil in your garden where it's safe for your dog to dig without disturbing your plants! This could also be in their own sandpit too.
Step 2 – Call your dog over to you and start poking around in the soil with your hand to get your dog's interest. They will likely be inquisitive and want to see what you are investigating.
Step 3 – Reward your dog with a treat if they nudge the soil with their nose to start with. Then reward even more so if they start to use their paws to move the soil.
NOTE: You can also push treats into the soil to encourage your dog to rummage through it if they are unsure what to do.
Step 4 – While your dog is digging, give them the cue 'Dig' and reward them. This way they'll be much more likely to repeat this behaviour in the future.

Enrichment Ideas For Dogs Who Love To Explore

Our dogs often lead somewhat sheltered lives, relying on us for how much of the world they are allowed to interact with. Getting out and exploring the world together will help you to improve the relationship you share with your dog and enrich their life in the process. New places mean new scents, sights, and sounds for your dog to explore, all of which give their brain some much-needed stimulation. Even dogs who are naturally a little more reserved, can benefit hugely from the opportunity to experience new scenarios. This will help to increase their confidence when faced with new things and will cement their trust in you too.

Here are some enrichment ideas for dogs who love to explore:

Novel Locations – Ideal for physical exercise, mental stimulation & exploring

Try and take your dog to new places to let them explore! Walking the same route every day will soon become boring, and your dog would love to explore the sights, sounds and scents of somewhere new if they were given the chance. So, if you usually do a road walk around the local area, why not see if there is a woodland or a secure dog-walking field nearby you could visit for a change? Even if you don't have something like that within easy access, simply walking a different route than usual, or stopping off somewhere new could be just what they need!

Interacting With The Environment – Ideal for: physical exercise, mental stimulation & exploring

Encourage your dog to really explore the environment they find themselves in. So, if they see a squirrel run up a tree in the woodland, it's okay to let them investigate the tree to see where the squirrel went. Or if your dog comes across a football team playing on the field where you are walking then let them watch it for a moment to see what is going on.

Something which can be really beneficial to create predictability for your dog is to provide them with 'Islands of Action.' Islands of Action are set places or points along your walking route where something fun always happens for your dog. So, for example, when you reach the top of the hill in the field you walk in regularly, your dog gets to enjoy a fun game of tug, you do some tricks they enjoy, or they get to go off-lead to run around. Whatever your dog enjoys and finds exciting and motivating, happens on your Islands of Action. Soon, your dog will know that something fun is about to happen on the approach to the island and this helps keep them focused on you because they know something great is about to happen!

NOTE: The safety of other animals and people is always paramount, so it's important they don't feel scared or are put in danger by your dog interacting with them. Always make sure you have your dog under close control when they are around people or wild animals. It's essential that your dog is never allowed to chase livestock. Even if your dog doesn't physically attack them, the stress of being chased can cause sheep and cows to abort their pregnancy and farmers are legally allowed to shoot dogs who are worrying their animals. So, it's vital everyone is kept safe.

Different Textured Surfaces – Ideal for: physical exercise, mental stimulation & exploring

Different textured surfaces are enriching for your dog. Try to factor in as many different textures onto your walks as possible. Look for; concrete pavements, long grassy meadows, crunchy leaves in a woodland, wet ground, uneven ground, mud, woodchip paths, gravel, shortly cut grass, cobbles, paving stones, spongey rubber tiles (often found in children's play areas) and as many other different types of surfaces you can think of. Even indoor surfaces like carpet, wood floor, laminate, stone, tiles, and lino etc. all offer some variation for your dog.

Paddling In A Stream/Swimming – Ideal for: physical exercise, mental stimulation & exploring

Not every dog is a naturally strong swimmer; some love water, while others prefer a little paddle through shallow streams. Most dogs will enjoy a cool splash in a stream with some encouragement. The feel of the water on their paws, paired with unusual textures adds some enrichment to your dog's daily walks.

It's also worth considering some hydrotherapy purely for your dog's enjoyment. Many owners think hydrotherapy is simply used for rehabilitation after injuries or surgery, but many hydrotherapy pools now offer 'fun' swims too. If your dog has been signed off by their vet as being healthy enough to attend a hydro session, then you should be good to go! Swimming helps to improve your dog's health and fitness levels, as well as giving their brain a workout too. And, because it is a non-weight-bearing exercise, even dogs who may struggle with joint issues are able to enjoy a good swim, which puts much less stress on their joints than long walks would.

Sensory Gardens – Ideal for: mental stimulation & exploring

You can create a sensory experience for your dog in your garden if you have one, or on a smaller scale inside your home too. The aim is to introduce your dog to lots of different scents, textures, sights, and tastes and encourage them to interact with them. Make sure that everything you choose to include is safe for your dog first, though! Some suggestions may include:

- Large logs or log slices placed around the garden for your dog to walk across. This improves their balance and adds interest for them.

- Large, smooth stones add a new texture for your dog to feel when they walk on them.
- Water features can make a fantastic addition to your garden as well as them being relaxing for your dog. If you have safe access to power outside, you could get an electric water feature, or a solar powered one if not.
- Woodchips or bark floor covering can create soft landings for dogs that love to jump around. However, some dogs may be tempted to eat it which can cause intestinal blockages, so avoid this if your dog is likely to swallow it.
- Different vantage points around the garden let your dog see the world from a different viewpoint. Railway sleepers, benches, chairs, or even mounds of grass can be great for giving your dog a different outlook.
- Old tyres can be useful additions to your sensory garden. They can be filled with sand or soil to create digging pits or used to plant herbs that you don't want to take over your garden. They are also great fun for your dog to jump on and off too, and their spongy texture will add some more interest for them as well.

When Enrichment Isn't Enriching

So, by now, you should have a good understanding of the importance of implementing enrichment activities into your dog's daily life. You will also have a clear idea of the types of enrichment that would be most beneficial for your dog, and how to provide them with these opportunities. Enrichment is a hugely positive addition to your dog's life and will undoubtedly improve their mental health and overall well-being. Your dog has everything to gain from regular enrichment opportunities and nothing to lose!

However, there are some things that can negatively impact the effectiveness of your chosen enrichment. Just because something should be enriching on paper, doesn't mean your dog will see it this way in reality. And remember, what one dog really enjoys, may not be enjoyable at all for another dog, so it is a process of trialling new things to see which have the most desirable effect. Here are some things that you need to consider when looking at the effectiveness of your enrichment activities:

There Are Scents Present That Your Dog Finds Undesirable

Synthetic scents like air fresheners, cleaning products, candles, and washing powder used for your dog's bedding can all be very undesirable for your dog. While they may smell appealing to us, they can be very overpowering to your dog's sensitive nose! So, if your dog suddenly loses interest in an enrichment activity they usually enjoy, it could be because their snuffle mat has been washed in something strong smelling and they now are reluctant to get their nose too close to it. Or, it could be that you have a new air freshener in the room, which is off-putting for your dog, making it harder for them to concentrate.

This also helps to explain why dogs who have been groomed and bathed in a strongly scented shampoo, will often want to go and roll in something 'gross' by our standards to try and rid themselves of their overpowering new scent. As much as we might want our dogs to smell like baby powder, or something that's pleasing to our human nose, chances are, they would much rather smell like fox poo or just plain doggy! So, it's best to avoid highly scented shampoos and opt for one containing natural ingredients that is low fragrance or fragrance-free.

There Are Too Many Distractions For Your Dog
Outside enrichment activities can be affected by the wind levels, temperature, weather conditions, sounds, and other distractions in the area which can all impact your dog's ability to concentrate on the task at hand. So, if your dog doesn't seem interested, or is becoming easily distracted, you can either make the exercise or activity easier for them to succeed in, or offer them something more exciting or engaging to do. This may hold their attention better.

However, even if you choose the most exciting enrichment activity, the distractions around them may still be too much for your dog to be able to concentrate, so in this instance it's best to try something different later on, when you are back in a low-distractive environment. For example, your dog may love a snuffle mat filled with treats when they are at home in your living room, but when they are out on a walk, they could be prioritising sniffing new scents of wildlife, other dogs, and people, more than sniffing out treats from their snuffle mat. This doesn't mean they have gone off this idea, it's more likely they don't find it enriching right now! Context is important when considering what is enriching for your dog and when.

Your Dog Is Living In A High-Stress Environment

While enrichment can be excellent at helping your dog to de-stress and relax, it can only go so far if your dog's environment is continually stressful for them. If your dog doesn't have time to fully decompress after stressful encounters, they can be reluctant to participate in enrichment activities. This is because their concentration levels will be lower, their tolerance levels will be decreased, and they are simply not in the right frame of mind for thinking, learning, or exploring.

In cases like this, your dog may be suffering from an issue known as 'trigger stacking.' This is when your dog runs into lots of stressful situations in quick succession, without any time to relax or decompress in between. This leads to them feeling more irritable, and less likely to enjoy certain enrichment activities that they usually like. It helps to imagine each stressful encounter as adding water to a cup, so if your dog feels anxious about being left alone, this adds water to their cup. Then, them not having a comfortable place to rest and relax adds a little more water. Then, someone knocks on the door meaning more water is added. Then lots of people are walking past your window which unsettles your dog and makes them bark, that's right, more water. This continues until there is no more room in your dog's glass for any more water and it overflows. Calming enrichment activities can help to drain some of this water from the cup, but if your dog is living in a way that creates more water to be added than is taken away, they will likely always be feeling on edge. Enrichment won't be as effective for a dog that is too stressed to focus on anything.

There Are Sounds Present That Your Dog Finds Intolerable

It's no secret that lots of dogs can struggle to deal with sudden or loud noises, and we always do our best to avoid exposing our dogs to these kinds of sounds. However, there are other sounds that your dog can hear, that you may not hear well at all. Things like sonar devices, are often used in products designed to scare away cats or wild birds from your garden. To your dog, these products will be emitting an extremely high-pitched screeching sound, which can make it impossible for them to concentrate and even reluctant to be anywhere near them at all.

If these sounds are present when your dog is participating in an enrichment activity, then they may begin to associate this activity with the unbearable sound they are hearing and not want to continue with it. So, this is something that should always be considered before purchasing products like this!

Many dogs are fearful of sudden loud noises like fireworks, so much so that they may refuse to participate in enrichment activities while the fireworks are happening. This is because they are simply to stressed or scared to concentrate, even if they usually enjoy the activity you are offering.

Your Dog Is Feeling Scared Or Overwhelmed
If your dog is flooded, scared, or over their tolerance threshold then they are not likely to be in the right headspace for enrichment. While some enrichment activities can be a good distraction for your dog, they will not relieve the underlying feeling of fear, stress, or anxiety your dog is feeling at that moment. Instead, give them plenty of time to calm down, and ideally remove whatever is causing their fear in the first place, to get the most out of your enrichment time.

NOTE: Flooding is when your dog is essentially 'thrown in at the deep end' and forced into a situation you know they will find scary and overwhelming. It is a very controversial training method for trying to deal with a dog's fear, as it can often make the situation much worse instead of improving it. So, if your dog is flooded and is completely overwhelmed, they will be in survival mode and will not be able to complete any enrichment effectively at this time.

Flooding is also referred to as 'immersion therapy' and it is often used in humans to help them deal with fears and phobias. However, the difference with humans is that they can give their express consent to be immersed in an environment they feel hugely uncomfortable in, to try and reap long-term benefits. An example would be agreeing to be locked into a room full of spiders, when they are your biggest fear in life. Our dogs have no choice or say in whether this is something they agree with or would benefit from, they are at our mercy for decisions like this and it is rarely in their best interests. A common example would be a dog who is nervous around other dogs being sent to a day care centre where they are surrounded by 20+ dogs to 'get them used to them.' Now, this will go one of two ways; 1. The dog will start behaving aggressively towards the other dogs because they are feeling overwhelmed, stressed, and desperate for them to give them some space. Or, 2. The dog will appear outwardly calm and submissive towards the other dogs, and this is the time where uneducated trainers/owners think 'the dog is fixed, look how calm they are around the other dogs now!' when in reality they are likely to be in state of learned helplessness.

Learned helplessness is actually one of the most heart-breaking things that can happen to your dog. This is when they learn through their experience, that nothing is going to get them out of this situation that they feel so desperately uncomfortable in, so they shut down and accept it, even though it's likely making them depressed and anxious. This is often the result of flooding or immersion therapy which begs the question of whether it is ethical to treat our sentient friends in this way?

Your Dog's Needs Are Not Being Met

If your dog's basic needs are not being met, they may feel hungry or thirsty, be in pain, etc. and if this is the case, then enrichment alone cannot improve those things and the effects of it will be diminished. Your dog's basic needs relate to the '5 Freedoms' which are; Freedom from hunger or thirst, Freedom from discomfort, Freedom from pain, injury, or disease, Freedom to express normal behaviour, and Freedom from fear and distress.

The '5 Freedoms' are all bare minimum essentials to maintain your dog's health and well-being and without them, these things are in jeopardy. Your dog's basic needs should always be fully fulfilled, and this should go without saying. And, this is where enrichment plays a fantastic part because it's core value is to encourage your dog's normal or natural behaviour. However, if the other areas of the 5 Freedoms are not being suitably covered, your dog won't get the most out of enrichment. It should all be considered holistically.

Your Dog Feels Forced To Participate In The Activity

If you are forcing your dog to participate in enrichment activities and it's not something they want to do, they won't be getting much from it. In the same way we might have been forced to run cross-country or solve difficult maths equations when we were at school, this doesn't mean we were getting any enjoyment out of these activities, we were just going through the motions because we didn't have a choice.

Enrichment is all about empowering your dog with the freedom to choose which will increase their confidence and improve their mental health. Forcing them to do something will be detrimental and have the opposite effect. And remember, just because we think something should be enriching for our dog, doesn't mean it automatically will be to this individual dog!

You Are Not Offering Enrichment Frequently Enough

Enrichment isn't a one-off thing. You will only get long-term effects and benefits if you implement these things long-term. Once the enrichment stops, so do the benefits. Dogs don't think to themselves 'oh, I remember two years ago when I was allowed to run off lead and I really enjoyed it, that felt really good!' They live much more in the moment than we do and can only process what is happening more recently and imminently to feel the benefits of this. Regular access to enrichment is key to your dog's happiness.

You Are Choosing The Wrong Kind Of Enrichment

Choosing the wrong type of activity for your dog's needs will only add frustration to their life, not enrichment. So, if your dog isn't able to run and jump, choosing to let them try flyball wouldn't add anything positive to their life. Not every dog will love every single enrichment idea found in this book, they will naturally have some they prefer and there will be some that suit some dogs more than others. The beauty is, there is something for everyone, so work together with your dog to find out what they enjoy most of all.

The Activity Is Too Difficult For Your Dog

Making the enrichment activity too difficult for your dog to work out leads to a build-up of frustration and stress and makes your dog want to give up. It can also make them less likely to want to try again in the future. The whole aim of enrichment is to increase your dog's confidence when they work out problems for themselves and this won't be possible if they don't stand a chance of working it out at all! This can also contribute towards your dog becoming unwilling to approach new things as openly because they are fearful of failure and frustration. This is the exact opposite of what we want to happen!

Nothing In Life Is Free Protocol

Some trainers actively encourage the idea that your dog should have to 'earn' every good thing they desire in life, this is known officially as the 'Nothing In Life Is Free' protocol. Some go as far as including everything a dog needs, including; food, treats, affection, praise, physical contact, play, access to resting places, access to the outdoors, and every other part of your dog's day-to-day life. The idea behind this protocol is that you get your dog to 'work' to gain access to all of these so-called privileges and without working for them, your dog won't receive them.

All this protocol does is give the human total control over their dog's entire existence. This ties in with the now de-bunked theory of dogs trying to be dominant and needing to know their place in the pack (aka your home) However, we now know scientifically that this is not the case and there is nothing to gain from trying to micromanage, control, and dominate your dog. All this will do is damage the relationship you share with each other and reduce the chance of you living harmoniously alongside each other.

However, it should be questioned whether ethically, it is fair for your dog to have to work for basic necessities like food, your attention, and access to places to rest? Whilst it is undoubtedly important to exercise your dog's mind and provide them with plenty of opportunities for mental stimulation, it's important not to get too carried away with this. Remember, enrichment should be adding something positive to your dog's life and should never be detrimental to their welfare.

If we look at a human example here, would you be happy to do 20 star jumps so you could have a conversation with a friend? Or, run around the block before you are allowed to eat your lunch? Even if you have answered yes to these questions, it's likely that the novelty of these activities would soon wear off! This would happen quickly, particularly when you consider that we can usually do these basic activities like chatting, eating, resting, socialising, etc, for 'free' without any prerequisites.

Therefore, I personally do not endorse the Nothing In Life Is Free protocol, as it's more likely to increase frustration for your dog, instead of adding enrichment.

Ditch The Bowl?
Some trainers suggest you ditch your dog's bowl entirely and use food toys, puzzles, and other enrichment activities to provide your dog with their daily food allowance. Now, this is a very divisive subject, with many arguing strongly for and against this idea. Whilst we know and understand the importance of getting your dog's brain thinking and providing them with an outlet for natural behaviours, however, if every single bit of food depends on this, then is this fair?

Our dogs are not naturally grazers, who eat little and often constantly throughout the day, so to be 'drip-fed' their daily food allowance throughout the entire day is not a particularly natural way for them to eat. It also never allows your dog to feel full, leaving them constantly either fully, or on the edge of being hungry. This is not a sustainable, long-term solution if you want to keep your dog happy and healthy. Granted, it will become monotonous and boring for your dog if they are only ever given their meals, in a bowl, twice a day, for their entire life. But, this is exactly why we need to introduce some enrichment activities too. I don't believe a dog bowl is the work of the devil (like some trainers do!) so before you ditch it entirely, consider your dog's needs first!

Frequently Asked Questions

You may still have some questions or concerns about enrichment that we haven't yet covered throughout the book. Hopefully, your questions will be answered in this chapter:

What If My Dog Doesn't Understand An Enrichment Activity?

This is not uncommon, especially if your dog hasn't had many opportunities for enrichment previously. The reality is, the more chances you give your dog to use their nose, their brain, and their body, the more confident they will become at trying new activities and working them out will become more desirable to them too. So, if your dog seems to be struggling with an activity in the beginning, help them! Make sure you always set them up for success, because as soon as your dog thinks something is too difficult, they may well give up trying to solve it at all, especially in the initial stages when their confidence and learning history are low. It's important therefore to make sure you start off any new activities at a very easy level for your dog, then only increase the difficulty once you are sure they have the hang of it.

Won't My Dog Gain Weight From The Extra Treats?

The simple answer to this is no, not if you are careful about how much they're eating! If you feed your dog their usual portions of food, plus lots of treats on top as part of enrichment activities, then yes, they are likely to gain weight which is detrimental to their long-term health and well-being. So, it's important you adjust the amount of food they're getting as their meals in relation to the amounts of treats they're consuming.

It's also worth considering the type of treats that you are using for your dog and avoid any that are highly processed as they often contain much higher levels of fat, sugar and salt which is unnecessary for your dog. Remember, some enrichment activities encourage your dog to move physically too, which is burning calories and not all of the activities rely on food! There are plenty that don't require extra treats at all.

I always recommend weighing out your dog's daily food portions to get a more accurate idea of exactly how much they are eating. This is more accurate than the 'handful measurement' which can be very hit-and-miss!

But My Dog Destroys Any Toys They're Given?

Okay, so, a lot of dogs love to chew up toys and some hardcore chewers can easily destroy 'indestructible' toys in a matter of minutes! I completely understand how this can become frustrating as an owner, especially if you are spending a lot of money on supposedly hard-wearing dog toys. However, a lot of dogs start to shred and destroy toys as a side effect of a build-up of excitement, tension, and frustration. They also see the toy as something that is bringing excitement and playtime and can easily get carried away and start to destroy it.

However, if you change the way that your dog interacts with the toy, you can help extend its longevity. Try to avoid just simply giving your dog the toy and leaving them to it, as this is often where the destructive behaviour really shines through. Because the toy isn't moving or doing anything exciting, your dog may want to add more interest to it by shredding it! Instead, try moving the toy around by dragging it across the floor and getting your dog to chase it, or throwing it across the ground for your dog to retrieve. Using the toy in several different ways adds more excitement to it and can reduce the risk of your dog being intent on destroying it!

It's also a good idea to follow a fun, high-intensity, game of fetch by giving them something they can shred afterwards. This could be an old toy that you don't mind being destroyed, or some treats wrapped in a paper bag which they can shred. This replicates the next part of the predatory sequence for your dog (dissection), which helps them to feel more satisfied and fulfilled after the thrill of the chase.

And remember, sometimes it is fun for your dog to simply shred up a toy and that's okay too! This is where teddies purchased from a charity shop are ideal. They cost less than toys made specifically for dogs, and if they get shredded then it's not a big deal!

What Time Of Day Should I Offer Enrichment?

The timing of your enrichment activities can affect how effective they can be for your dog and how much interest they show in completing them. For example, if you offer your dog a snuffle mat directly after they have eaten a meal, they may not be as motivated to search for the treats because they are already feeling full and don't desire food as much at that moment. It's also not a good idea to do any enrichment activities that include physical exercise directly after your dog has eaten, as this can increase the chance of the developing GDV, or bloat, which can be life-threatening if left untreated. So, avoid activities like fetch, or flirt poles for example, when your dog has just eaten.

It's also worth noting that your dog can react differently to enrichment activities depending on if you offer them during daylight hours or in the dark. Because your dog cannot see as well in low light, they are likely to be naturally more tentative when approaching new things. This explains why some dogs may bark or be apprehensive around things in the dark that they are usually comfortable with when they see them during daylight. So, it's best to stick with activities your dog already knows and are comfortable with if they are more uncertain about being in the dark.

Will Enrichment Encourage My Dog To Be Destructive?

No! Absolutely not! The whole point of enrichment is to give your dog a suitable and safe outlet for their natural canine behaviours. So, instead of them chewing up your furniture, they have toys to play with and activities to get their brain working. Just because you have given your dog a toilet roll tube to shred up in an enrichment activity, doesn't mean they will automatically steal a full toilet roll from the bathroom for shredding. It's all about context. The toilet roll tube you give to your dog contains treats and the whole motive of the game is for your dog to access the treats, if they destroy the tube in the process, this is a side effect of the bigger picture. So, when your dog sees the full toilet roll hanging up in the bathroom, they won't link this to the one you provide them with that's filled with treats. In the same way as they won't beg for food from a clean plate in your kitchen cupboard, as it's not really the plate they are interested in at all, this is just something that holds the food that they want to get their paws on.

If anything, enrichment can go a long way to preventing destructive behaviours from your dog, because their need to chew, shred, bark, dig, run etc are all being met through the enrichment activities you are providing them with, so they don't need to find their own outlet for them elsewhere.

My Dog Does The Activities Too Quickly?
If your dog is whizzing through a certain activity, you can either increase the difficulty level, or try something totally new. Many owners want a single enrichment activity to last for many hours, which is particularly common when dogs need to be left alone and you want to keep them busy. However, a

lot of the time, the enjoyment your dog is getting from their enrichment is amplified when you work together as a team. So, it's quite unrealistic to expect any enrichment activity to last for hours on end as this is not really what their intention is. The aim is to give your dog something interesting and engaging to do, and if this continued for hours, you are likely to be adding frustration and tension to your dog and they may well give up entirely if they feel like it's too hard for them to succeed.

It's also important to note that just because your dog does a particular enrichment activity several times, doesn't mean they will get bored of it. Yes, they likely know what to do and how to solve it pretty quickly, but they still get that feeling of happiness and contentment every time they participate in it. So, feel free to use a snuffle mat several times a week, or play treat bowling each day, or go through tricks your dog already knows.

What If My Dog Isn't Interested In Food?

A lot of owners think their dog isn't interested in food when in reality you probably just haven't found what really motivates your dog yet. It can be helpful to write a list of treats which your dog really loves on a scale of 1-5. With number one being something they go absolutely wild for! It's not hard to see why your dog may not be interested in their kibble being placed in a puzzle toy, when this is something they are given every day in their bowl for 'free' so why should they work any harder to access it? However, when faced with some cooked chicken, you may find they are more likely to want to investigate that and snuffle through a snuffle mat or the grass to find it. This works for 3 reasons; Firstly, because this is not something they have access to freely on a day-to-day basis, so they value it more highly. Secondly, this is much tastier to your dog than their normal food or cooked treat biscuits. And thirdly, they have a much stronger scent profile which is much more enticing and interesting for your dog. Even after these types of treats have already been eaten, the scent of them remains around the area for much longer than dried foods, encouraging your dog to keep investigating for longer.

So, when you are considering the types of treats you are offering to your dog, think about these factors to help you choose. Tasty treat ideas include; tuna, grated cheese, cooked meats, sardines, spread cheese, pate, etc.

What If I Can't Afford To Purchase Enrichment Toys?

There really is no need to purchase specialist enrichment toys for your dog unless you would really like to! Enrichment shouldn't feel like a competition where you are comparing yourself to other dog owners who have more/better/fancier enrichment equipment than you do. In fact, I would argue that homemade options take even more thought and attention to put together than a shop-bought item. It brings out your creative side and can often lead to you thinking of other ideas to help bring some joy to your dog's life.

There are loads of different enrichment ideas within this book and more, that revolve around homemade games or activities, or just spending quality time with your dog. And, you don't need to spend any money on these things!

Is My Dog Getting Frustrated?
There is a very fine line between your dog thinking and problem-solving, and them becoming frustrated. As we have already mentioned earlier in the book, there is no harm in giving your dog a helping hand with an activity if you think they are struggling or getting frustrated by it. In fact, this can actually be beneficial to your relationship, as your dog will soon learn that they can look to you and rely on you to help if they find themselves in a situation they are struggling with. Teamwork makes the dream work! Cheesy but true!

But My Dog Isn't Interested In Enrichment Activities At All?
If you feel like your dog is uninterested in enrichment, then it may be the case that you simply have come across something that they find really enjoyable yet. Really think about your dog's breed and what makes them tick. Do they like digging up your garden? Then check out the section for dogs who love to dig. Maybe they like to chase squirrels in the park? Then take a look at the section for dogs who love to chase. Although chasing squirrels and digging up your garden may not be desirable behaviours to us, it's important that we offer our dogs the opportunity to display these behaviours in

a safe way. This is exactly what enrichment is all about!

Some owners think that their dog is too 'lazy' or 'can't be bothered' to do anything like this. However, just because your dog is quietly lying on the floor by your feet as you read this, doesn't automatically mean that they wouldn't benefit from a quick bit of enrichment. While they don't need to be 'on-the-go' all the time, your dog is much more capable of getting their brain into gear than you might think!

What If I Don't Have Time To Provide Enrichment?

Many owners are worried that they simply don't have time to provide their dog with any enrichment. And it's true that many households are busy and time poor. However, you may be surprised at just how many little opportunities go unnoticed during the day. For example, instead of sticking to the same route when you walk your dog, try walking it backwards, or walking somewhere new entirely. This still gets your dog walk done but makes it more interesting for your dog (and for you!)

Or, when you finally sit down to watch TV, give your dog a puzzle toy to work out. This lets you unwind on the sofa and gives your dog some mental stimulation without a huge amount of input from you.

Really try to think hard about the amount of time you can commit to enrichment activities. We owe it to our dogs to give them as many opportunities as possible to behave in a natural way. Slowly but surely, these slight changes will become second nature to you, and you will soon be offering your dog these opportunities without even realising, despite you thinking that you don't have time to do so.

Here are some suggestions of how to filter enrichment into your busy schedule:

You are already:	How you can enrich this:
Feeding your dog from their bowl twice a day	Try using a snuffle mat, scatter feeding, lick mat or puzzle toy occasionally
Walking your dog on the same daily route	Go on a Sniffari or explore a new route together
Purchasing toys for your dog to play with	Try wrapping the new toy before giving it to your dog or choosing a new toy which makes sounds
Chilling out on the sofa watching TV with your dog	See if they would like some gentle massage, or a natural treat to chew on
Weeding your garden	Teach your dog to dig on cue so they can help you dig the borders!
Tidying the house	Teach your dog to put your recycling in the bin or pick your clothes up off the floor and into the washing basket
Giving your dog a treat	Try hiding the treats around the house or garden and encouraging your dog to sniff them out

Making small adjustments to the things you are already doing in your day, will help to make your dog's life more enriched, without much more commitment from you.

Can I Give My Dog Too Much Enrichment?
Technically, there isn't really too much of a good thing when it comes to enrichment. As we now understand, it's hugely beneficial to use enrichment techniques as often as we can to help our dogs lead happier lives. However, what I will say is that it's important that you vary the type of enrichment that your dog is offered. For example, let's say your dog's favourite activity is a snuffle mat. They won't want to continually use a snuffle mat for hours on end. They will reach a point where they don't really want to eat any more treats, and they are feeling tired from the constant sniffing and exploring. So, it's better to let them enjoy their snuffle mat until they are finished, then perhaps follow this up with a long-lasting chew to help them unwind further.

Can I Use Enrichment Instead Of Physical Exercise?
Some trainers suggest that you can use enrichment activities in exchange for physical exercise entirely. However, this is not strictly sound advice for the vast majority of dogs. It's important you maintain a healthy level of physical exercise for your dog, as well as giving them plenty of enrichment opportunities. These two things bring different elements to your dog's life, happiness, and well-being so it's important that one is not favoured over

the other. Physical exercise is imperative for a healthy body and enrichment is imperative for a healthy mind. These two should intertwine, and not exclude each other.

Conclusion

It's our duty to provide enrichment for our dogs as they are often trapped in a world that they are trying hard to navigate alongside humans who can rarely communicate with them effectively. The stress and anxiety that this can cause for our dogs can sometimes be immediately apparent but often it lurks under the surface. And your dog has to battle this alone, often without you knowing.

The lives of wolves and other wild canids like Dingoes are full of unlimited amounts of stimuli to which our dogs either have no or very limited access to. Instead, they now rely on us for every aspect of their care, and enrichment should form a large part of this responsibility. Although our dogs are not wild, they are fully domesticated, and their lives are now totally different to their wild ancestors, this further cements their need for mental stimulation even more solidly.

Therefore, enrichment shouldn't be seen as an optional extra when it comes to sharing your life with these sentient beings. It should be an essential addition to your dog's life to ensure their happiness and well-being. And, the added bonus is that it will improve your life too, as well as the relationship between you and your dog.

The sheer importance of enrichment for our canine companions is still not fully appreciated by everyone, but I hope that as you are now reaching the end of this book you will have a new-found desire to enrich your dog's life as much as you possibly can and, have the tools to implement this effectively.

Hopefully, at this stage, you will have learned:

- The importance of giving your dog choices and agency over their life and their environment
- The true benefits of enrichment and how it has the potential to change your dog's life for the better
- How much better your relationship with your dog will become, if you make a conscious effort to improve their life
- How to change your mindset to view your dog's behaviour as part of a bigger picture and not just as a nuisance
- How your dog's breed and personality can affect the type of enrichment activity they would enjoy and get the most out of
- The importance of enrichment being something you provide to your dog as often as possible, throughout their whole life
- Over 50+ fantastic enrichment activities for you to try with your own dog

So, what are you waiting for? Now you have all of this new-found knowledge and information swirling around your brain, start putting it to use and begin enriching your dog's life.

Encourage them to be their true, authentic selves. Give them an outlet for their intrinsic needs. Let them behave more naturally than our human-world often allows them to.

Our dogs deserve it.

Extract From 'Canine Contentment'

Canine Contentment is the first book of the 'Help Your Dog Be Happier' series by Charlotte Garner. It's aim is to help teach people how a holistic approach to your dog's well-being, is the best way to achieve complete contentment for them. Here's an extract from the introduction to get you started:

Introduction

Our dogs are sentient beings who have the ability to form strong bonds with us as humans, and in turn, they look to us to provide them with everything they require to lead a happy and fulfilled life. A good starting point for what your dog requires in order for them to live comfortably, can be found outlined in the 'Five Freedoms,' which details a list of five basic requirements that all dogs should be provided with.

The standards included in this list are not only something all our dogs should have as a minimum; they are also a legality in UK law under the Animal Welfare Act of 2006. So, failure to provide them effectively is considered a criminal offence. The 'Five Freedoms' are as follows;

- **Freedom from hunger and thirst -** through the provision of easily accessible clean water and an appropriate diet to maintain optimum health

- **Freedom from pain, injury, disease or illness** - through rapid diagnosis and treatment of any suspected health issues
- **Freedom to express normal, species appropriate behaviours** - through providing a suitable living environment, appropriate facilities and the company of the animal's own kind if this is appropriate to their individual needs
- **Freedom from discomfort** - through providing a comfortable resting area and shelter from the outside elements
- **Freedom from fear or distress** - through ensuring that the conditions in which they live and the treatment that they receive do not cause any mental distress or suffering

These freedoms are all a very basic minimum for any animal, and if you are unable or unwilling to provide these for them, then you should really be questioning your suitability for dog ownership.

However, I would hope that all of you that have found yourselves here, are already providing these things subconsciously for your dogs, as they are based on simply showing kindness. Ensuring all of these outlines are met, will, of course, go some way towards your own dog feeling content.

This book will provide you with a more detailed outline of how to ensure your dog is the happiest they can possibly be, far exceeding the limits of these guidelines. So, if you wish to know exactly how to achieve complete canine contentment with your own dog at home, then you have found yourself in the right place. This book will provide you with all the information and advice you require, to not only improve your relationship with your dog, but also how to enhance their lives and make sure that their happiness and well-being are continuous.

I understand all too well how owners are often frustrated by their dog's behaviour and the fact that they simply do not know how to remedy the issues they are facing. This is commonly caused because of a lack of understanding of what may be causing the issues in the first instance.

The journeys that I have shared with my own current dogs, combined with working professionally with dogs for the past several years, have culminated in the advice and information I will share with you here.

We will discuss many different aspects of dog ownership in turn, and then discover how they all work harmoniously together in relation to your dog's happiness and contentment. Your dog's diet, the amount of exercise they receive, the training methods you use to teach them new skills, the enrichment activities they are provided with, and the socialisation they experience, all play their own key roles in ensuring your dog's happiness.

We shall also explore how being able to analyse your dog's body language effectively will help you to better understand their communication. Then finally, we will discover the truth behind some common misconceptions and myths surrounding our dogs, with the aim of providing you with a clearer understanding of the dog you share your life with.

By increasing your understanding of your dog's exact needs through reading this book, I am positive that this will result in not only an improved, strengthened relationship between you, but also a calmer, happier and more contented dog overall too. Therefore, I would encourage you to read the book as a whole, as I am passionate in my belief in a more wholesome approach to canine behaviour, welfare and contentment. Choosing this approach, as opposed to focusing solely on individual aspects, helps you to create better, longer-lasting results.

Think of this as an adventure that you are sharing with your dog by your side, as you travel down this road of discovery together, and in the process, you will strengthen the bond you share with each other, and improve their lives along the way.

Don't feel guilty if there are things you discover here that you have not previously considered, we are all on a constant learning journey, so we should always be open to new opportunities to further enhance our dog's life, based on the knowledge we currently have. Just the fact that you have purchased this book is the first step in the right direction and proves that you are already in the mindset of wanting to help your dog to be happier, which is amazing in itself!

Instead of feeling overwhelmed at the extent of the possible changes and additions you feel would benefit your dog, simply gradually add them in one by one and watch as your dog reaps the benefits. Achieving canine contentment is not a race; it is a lifelong project that you and your dog can actively work together on. It is not as straightforward as just working through each of the contents of the chapters here and saying you have completed it. There will be many different twists and turns on the road ahead of you, so be prepared to work hard to maintain your dog's happiness throughout their various life stages.

We must always be sure to remember, that we choose to bring a dog into our lives, and all too often we expect them to just slot into our routine, without properly considering their needs, which is where many behavioural issues can stem from. Unfortunately, in many circumstances, it is rarely as easy as simply choosing a dog, bringing them home and then living happily ever after. However, with the right guidance, information, and kind methods, this can become much more of a reality than a fairy-tale. This is where 'Canine Contentment – The Essential Guide' steps in...

Enjoy!

Canine Contentment by Charlotte Garner is available as an e-book, paperback (ISBN 979-8709399082) and hardcover (ISBN 979-8763067781)

Extract From 'Rocket Recall'

Rocket Recall is by Simone Mueller and is part of her Predation Substitute Training series of books. It's aim is to teach owners how to achieve a reliable 'rocket recall' with their own dog using positive methods. Here's an extract to get you started:

Why Do So Many Dog Owners Struggle With Their Dog's Recall?

A reliable recall is one of the greatest challenges for many dog owners. But why is that so?

First of all, we need to understand that a recall is something aversive - negative - that is happening to the dog. It's something that goes against what they actually want to do in the moment. When we use a recall, we're asking them to turn away and abandon something that they are interested in, or something they want to check out.

Turning away from that interesting smell, person, animal, or other distraction and having to come back to us is the first "disappointment" for the dog. We naturally try to "make up" for this disappointment by giving them a treat, but often, the treat is not really a reward for our dog. Why is this? It's because the treat doesn't fulfill a need that they feel at that moment. Giving a treat is not functional - it's not part of an understood system driven by their instincts - and it can become a second "disappointment" during the recall.

Let's look at it another way, for clarity. Think back and remember the way you felt as a child when a parent called you inside for dinner, but the other kids you were with kept on playing. While you likely enjoyed eating as a normal activity, in this situation, it wasn't what you actually wanted to do. You wanted to remain playing with your friends! You may have even perceived it as a kind of punishment, as you had to leave your friends behind. You felt disappointed, sad, maybe even angry that you had to abandon what you wanted to do, even though it was for something else that you typically enjoyed.

A dog that turns away from chasing a cat, or playing with another dog, might feel the same way, even if we offer them a treat. Even though your dog loves to eat at home and in a non-distracting environment, they might not perceive that same treat as a reward when outside the home. Believe it or not, this is one of the reasons why so many dogs are hesitant or even resistant to taking treats outside.

Exploring the idea of "disappointments" within a recall further, some dog owners struggle with their dog's recall because they consciously or unconsciously punish their dog for coming back. This may look like:

1. A prior loss of temper and subsequent yelling at a "naughty" dog that slipped their lead or got out.

2. A waiver or hardness to your voice, born out of fear that they won't come back the last few steps or may dart into the road.
3. Your body language and stance changing to a threatening one when you're preparing to chase your dog down as they turn away.

Even if you don't remember doing any of these things exactly, human nature dictates you're likely guilty of at least one at some point. It was when this happened that your dog may have started to associate your recall with something negative or punitive - the "disappointment." You recalled your dog from something interesting, put them on lead, or called them away from their friends and ended the fun. According to learning theory, this is punishment.

A final familiar reason why dogs struggle to come back is a lack of training. They may understand what a recall is functionally, in the moment, but not that recall means recall regardless of the situation. Their owners have trained their recall at home, or in a similar non-distracting environment, but neglected to instill proper generalisation of the cue. In order to generalise the cue properly, you'll need to repeat it hundreds, even thousands, of times in various situations and alongside different distractions.

In order to set our dogs up for success we need to carefully structure these situations and scaffold the distractions, allowing us to work through them in a kind of "bucket list" for our dogs. In this holistic training program, we will tackle all three of the common issues that cause dog owners to struggle with their dog's recall: the reluctance to abandon something interesting, a feeling of punishment, and a lack of training. We'll also learn how to make a reward functional, ensuring it has the intended effect on your dog and doesn't feel like a disappointment.

Throughout this training, you will play games with your dog that rewire their brain, ensuring that coming back to you is no longer a punishment. Once you've properly implemented these techniques, in fact, they'll actually feel the desire to come back to you. We'll also work together to create a well-structured and scaffolded bucket list of distractions, situations, and reward options to work through.

Let's get started!

Rocket Recall by Simone Mueller is available as an e-book, paperback (ISBN 9978-3982187815) and hardcover (ISBN 979-8753195760)

About The Author

Charlotte has been immersed in the animal world from her very early childhood and was lucky enough to grow up surrounded by a vast menagerie of pets including; cats, guinea pigs, hamsters, rabbits, chickens, fish, horses and of course, dogs!
Her love of dogs became so strong, in fact, that at the age of 11, she actually borrowed a local dog trainer's dogs, in order to attend obedience and agility classes with them, as she did not currently have a dog of her own! It is here where she was introduced to positive reinforcement training, and so her dog training obsession began.

This arrangement continued for around 3 years, which provided Charlotte with time to gain invaluable skills and experience through working with these dogs, as well as offering the opportunity for her to regularly compete in agility, breed shows and obedience competitions all over the country. It was then, that her trainer and mentor organised for her to have a dog of her own, in the form of Sky, a Border Collie puppy, who is featured on the books front cover. After all, she is the dog that started it all!

Fast forward a couple of years later, to when Charlotte and her Mum set up their own foster-based dog rescue, subsequently acquiring a further 3 dogs in the process, Tizzy, Inka and then later Delta, who make up the current dogs that Charlotte shares her life with today, each of whom have taught her countless lessons of their own.

Over the years that the rescue was in operation, they helped to successfully rehome over 600 dogs to their forever homes, which was not only a huge achievement, but also provided Charlotte with numerous opportunities to work with dogs from a whole host of different backgrounds, broadening her experience further still.

Charlotte's love of animals and thirst for knowledge then led her to go on to qualify as a Veterinary Care Assistant, then furthermore gain a diploma in Canine Behaviour, enabling her then to set up her own business offering 1-2-1 canine behaviour consultations, as well as group classes for puppies and adult dogs.

Currently, Charlotte is a freelance writer about all things dog-related! Not only has she previously written her first book, 'Canine Contentment – The Essential Guide' and now this book, she also regularly writes for Edition Dog Magazine and has co-written a second book 'Don't Eat That!' alongside Simone Mueller. She is still as passionate today as ever, about improving the relationship between dogs and owners and, in turn, ensuring that our dog's lives are happier and more contented.

She describes this book as being 'something I have been wanting to share with the world for a while now. I understand first-hand how important enrichment is to our dog's lives, and I would love to encourage as many people as possible to intertwine it into their dog's life too. My love and passion for dogs are so strong, so I am keen to share my knowledge and ethics with the rest of the world. I would love to help as many people as possible make sure that their dogs are happy, loved and well taken care of.'

Connect With The Author

If you have enjoyed reading my book and would like to keep in touch, you can find me on:

Facebook: Charlotte Garner - Canine Author
Instagram: @charlottegarnercanineauthor
Email: canineauthor@yahoo.com
Website: www.charlotte-garner.com

If you have purchased this book through Amazon, I would really appreciate you leaving me a review on there too, once you have finished reading it.

Or, if you are reading the Kindle edition, I would appreciate you leaving me a star rating.

I would love to see photos of the lovely dogs you share your lives with and how this book may have benefitted them, so please feel free to send them to me via social media or email.

Or, if you have any further questions about enrichment, please ask me!

Thank you

Charlotte

Made in the USA
Las Vegas, NV
21 April 2023

70929974R00100